P9-BYX-962

30

DAYS TO
YOUR BEST
MARRIAGE

PUBLISHING GROUP

NASHVILLE, TENNESSEE

Copyright © 2016 by B&H Publishing Group
All rights reserved.
Printed in the United States of America

978-1-4336-4571-6

Published by B&H Publishing Group
Nashville, Tennessee

Dewey Classification: 306.81
Subject Heading: MARRIAGE \ DOMESTIC
RELATIONS \ COMMUNICATION IN MARRIAGE

Unless otherwise noted, all Scripture is taken from Holman
Christian Standard Bible (HCSB), copyright © 1999, 2000,
2002, 2003, 2009 by Holman Bible Publishers,
Nashville Tennessee. All rights reserved.

Also used: King James Version (KJV)
which is public domain.

1 2 3 4 5 6 7 8 • 21 20 19 18 17 16

Contents

Introduction

You are really to be congratulated for picking up a book like this. Most people, if they're reading anything at all today, are probably caught up in a new novel or simply following along with whatever's trending on the best-seller list. (Nothing wrong with that, of course.) But you've decided instead to invest a little something extra into your marriage, and that's a pursuit that's got the will of God written all over it.

So we'll trust His Spirit to take these brief, thematic chapters and personally direct you toward at least a handful of key changes that could make some huge differences in your relationship. For the better. Or better yet, for the best. The best ever.

This book is not heavily prescriptive. Not a lot of do-this ideas. Your marriage, like others, is in too unique of a place and season to be reduced to a global list of 1-2-3 strategies. But as you spend a few minutes with these daily readings, hopefully your strategy list will sort of populate itself. You'll recognize the places where you've allowed your marriage to slip away from what you always intended, and you'll volunteer to be the one who starts putting it back where it belongs.

Read alone. Read together. Zoom through it over a weekend, or take it once a day for a whole month . . . or for however long it takes. Just know you've made a good choice by giving your wife or husband everything you've got, all over again.

Day 1

God First, God Always

What's Most Important

Seek first the kingdom of God and His righteousness, and all these things will be provided for you. (Matthew 6:33)

You came here, obviously, looking to invest some set-aside time into your marriage. That's great. What we find, however, is that no matter *what* we're seeking to improve, enhance, refresh, or even to rescue—whether our marriage, our work, our schedule, or our golf game—there is always only one best place to start. And we can say it like this: *We dedicate these next thirty days to the Lord.*

Let's be serious, not sanctimonious, when we say that. Because He is not supposed to be the main subject only at church. And at Easter. He is not just God for those moments when we single Him out for special attention, or when we

3

know we're in over our head with a particular situation and are needing to call in the heavy artillery.

He is God first.

And He is God always.

He is where we begin, or else we will not end up where we intended to go.

So in case you were ready to dive right into the number one, hot-topic issue on your marriage radar today . . . *you are!* And by the time we actually dial that one up—the one that's most on your mind right now—you'll be so glad you decided to go directly to God first instead of directly into what appears to be your most pressing agenda item.

The Bible is littered with some pretty major examples of people wanting to get moving with the action of their lives rather than putting God first from the start. The ancient children of Israel, you'll recall, after being delivered from bondage in Egypt, showed a real penchant for this kind of impatience—none more grievous than at the base of Mount Sinai while Moses was meeting face-to-face with God. The Lord had appeared on the mountain amid thunder and smoke, calling Moses to ascend into His holy presence for the receiving of the law. The whole scene had left the awesome impression that something of major significance was happening there. But when Moses, in the people's estimation, was "delayed in coming down from the mountain" (Exod. 32:1), some of their on-the-ground leadership decided God was just slowing down the operation. That's when they constructed the golden calf, foolishly thinking the god it represented could speed things along toward that land of milk and honey they'd been hearing about.

Year later, King Saul, trying to fend off the pesky Philistines, had been told ahead of time to wait for Samuel in a certain city, where this spiritual leader of Israel would offer sacrifices and give him further direction from God. But Samuel—again, in the people's estimation—hadn't shown up quickly enough to suit them (1 Sam. 13:11–12). And so, pressuring Saul, they intimidated him into rolling ahead with that burnt offering business on his own. With disastrous consequences for his future as king.

Here's the lesson to learn from this: If we want to do things right, we start in the right place—by putting God in *first* place.

That's what Nehemiah did. As a Jewish exile serving the Persian king, he became grief-stricken one day when his brother arrived from their Israelite homeland, fresh with news of the struggles their people were enduring. The city lay in ruins, its walls and former glories broken down. Nehemiah, after prayerfully petitioning the king, was given royal permission to lead a work group there to rebuild the infrastructure that had fallen victim to marauders and general decay.

The first thing he noticed on arrival, after making a crash inspection, was the enormity of the task before him, against all kinds of enemy opposition. There was a whole lot to do, and no time to lose. But if anything good was going to come from their efforts, it would only happen by first believing "the God of heaven is the One who will grant us success" (Neh. 2:20).

So as an opening statement to this enormous action plan, delegated among hundreds of volunteers, designed to restore the entire wall-and-gate structure around the historic city of Jerusalem—home to a proud nation's hearts—"Eliashib the high priest . . . began rebuilding the Sheep Gate. They dedicated it and installed its doors. After building the wall to the Tower of the Hundred and the Tower of Hananel, they dedicated it" (3:1).

They dedicated it.

This was God's . . . glory to His name. And by recognizing Him as their beginning point, they knew He would bless the work of their hands with His favor.

So right here on Day 1 of this brief little season of devotional time, concentrated specifically on your marriage, let's begin where all great endeavors should begin. Let's dedicate these experiences wholeheartedly to Him, believing that His plans and desires for us and our marriages go beyond even our own highest hopes.

You may look at your relationship and see *this* that needs fixing, *this* that's causing trouble, an aggravation you're getting *soooo* frustrated having to handle, something that the two of you always seem to be fighting about. A problem with *him*, a problem with *her* (and, okay, maybe a few problems with *you* as well). But by starting with your attention fixed firmly on God, rather than focusing it so fiercely on the usual suspects, your universe of possible solutions becomes as broad as His eternal love and power, not just the tired extent of your bright ideas.

We dedicate these next thirty days to You, Lord. And we wait to see what our marriages could start to look like by then.

Day 2

You Promised

Remembering Your Vows

*I will fulfill my vows to the LORD in the
presence of all His people. (Psalm 116:18)*

One thing we know for sure: the day when a couple speaks their marriage vows to one another at the altar—that's not the day when they really need those promises to matter. I mean, hey, they're in love; they're excited; they've been planning and awaiting this moment for a long, long time. So *of course* I'll have and hold you from this day forward, for better, for worse, for richer, for poorer, in sickness and in health, to love and to cherish . . .

All that stuff feels a million miles away.

But those vows, spoken before family and friends and God Almighty in that hour . . . they're not really for that hour. They're for a cold hour one wintry morning, seven or eight years later, when the chill outside can't even compare to the icy conditions in your hallways and shared living spaces. Who knows how it got to this point, what happened to bring it about? Something became three things, became an accumulation of things, and now there's not *anything*—even if it's a "sky is blue" statement of fact—that the two of you can seem to agree on.

Marriage vows are also for a late-night hour ten years later when fatigue is high and temptation is beckoning— the sizzle of a thrilling adventure, or maybe just a getaway escape, something to relieve the stress and pressure. They're for a dull, midday hour many years afterward, when love and commitment drip with the ooze of our spouse's surgical dressings and with spoonfuls of thin soup, guided gently from hand to mouth.

That's when we find out if those vows we made were just the traditional wordings people say or if they were true promises we intend to keep. They don't really matter until those moments when our honeymoon isn't what's coming up next. Moments when a pouty little face can't be easily nudged back into a smile by a playful tickle in the ribs and a "come on, don't be mad at me." Moments when those odd traits we used to think were kind of cute and quirky in our wife's or husband's harmless little way . . . they're not so funny anymore.

Vows. Promises.

To love him, to love her, forever.

"Fulfill what you vow," said the writer of Ecclesiastes. "Better that you do not vow than that you vow and not fulfill it" (Eccles. 5:4–5). The Bible—the Word—clearly communicates the gravity of the words we speak and what they're supposed to mean. God said to His earliest people, as part of His law, "If you make a vow to the LORD your God, do not be slow to keep it, because He will require it of you, and it will be counted against you as sin" (Deut. 23:21). "Be careful to do whatever comes from your lips, because you have freely vowed what you promised to the LORD your God" (v. 23). Jesus, whose words were always grounded and purposeful, said "that on the day of judgment people will have to account for every careless word they speak. For by your words you will be acquitted, and by your words you will be condemned" (Matt. 12:36–37).

These words we say . . .

They matter. They mean something.

We've been brought up in a culture of apology. "Sorry." "Oops." "I can explain that." "Won't happen again." And certainly the rub of human interaction, when irritated by human weakness, will always require the give-and-take of apology and forgiveness if we're to keep from entirely rubbing out the whole population. The gospel, too, and its ongoing process of sanctification in our lives, invites a response of admitted guilt, of forthcoming confession, of second chances punctuated by a deep-hearted desire for repentance. We do, we must live by being able through God's grace to recover from where we've failed.

But *sorry* is not the magic word for every situation. Nor is it the building block of trust and unity. Although apology is often unfortunately necessary, some of the blessings that God intends for our marriages are sure to spiral away from us if we're a continuous roundabout of what we meant to do, but didn't do, and wished we'd done, and want to do over.

When was the last time you looked back at your wedding tape (if you have one) or reviewed in print the spoken vows you made in one candlelit moment to that man, to that woman, to whom you were promising the rest of your life? Perhaps your vows were the standard issue variety—the longstanding basics that have lived throughout the long history of the church. Perhaps you went the nontraditional route, even writing your own, personalizing them to the unique qualities of your unique relationship. But in either and all cases, you made some promises that day. *Vows.* (Let's call them *vows*, to use a weightier word.) And though you couldn't possibly understand everything they entailed—none of us do—you made those vows for a day just like today. For a boring day. A routine day. A day when you didn't sleep well last night and didn't have your coffee this morning. A day when that wife or husband of yours did something to tick you off so bad that you really don't know how much more of this you can take.

"From this day forward," you said . . . "for better, for worse, for richer, for poorer, in sickness and in health, to love and to cherish, until death parts us."

Did you really mean that? What you said?

Today would be the best judge of that.

Day 3

Keeping It Real
Managing Expectations

*If anyone wants to come with Me, he
must deny himself, take up his cross
daily, and follow Me. (Luke 9:23)*

We know enough not to expect the dreamland portrayal of marriage to actually happen. We realize people whose lives seem as if they have it . . . no, actually they don't. They may have a *good* marriage, a *healthy* marriage, but not a mystically magical marriage. The view from the outside is probably quite different from the view on the inside. There's no such thing as easy street, and no wife or husband would ever have given us our way every time we wanted it.

But since those kinds of expectations are so far out of the realm, they are not the ones that actually give us the most trouble. The ones that retain the power to inflict delusional damage on us are those we've borrowed from others' real lives and tried to force fit onto our own.

For example, our ideal of the perfect marriage may be the one our *parents* have (if it's been a good one). We covet the kind of marriage our *friends* have (especially in those particular areas where we don't have it). We want the marriage where our husband doesn't need to be reminded to check the leak under our car, and where our wife truly understands what the first weekend of deer season means to a man. We want the marriage where our husband capably takes the lead as spiritual leader in our home, and where our wife doesn't treat the kids as if they can't do anything for themselves. We want the marriage where we can get away with making a mess, and where somebody will probably clean it up for us.

We've got this picture in our heads, see, of what marriage is supposed to be—and of what we think it actually *could* be if our spouse would just cooperate a little, if they'd understand we're not being unreasonable to expect it. We've also got this picture of what God is supposed to do so that we don't need to put up with some of the stuff that's keeping us from having what we always thought our married life would be. Why *can't* we have it that way? Like *they* do? Whoever *they* are.

But our expectations, although maybe not the fairy-tale variety, still may not be those that are viable in the real world.

Jesus came across a lot of people who carried unreasonable expectations of what belief in Him entailed. Somebody would approach Him, wanting to tag along as one of His followers. This looked like a lot of fun, they figured, or at least seemed to scratch their itch for developing a deeper sense of purpose in their lives. They wanted to join on with a cause, the way a young kid might want to sign up at the army recruitment office. *See the world. Be somebody's hero.* They wanted to be part of something bigger than themselves. Sure beat working this boring old job.

"I will follow You wherever You go!" one of them said (Luke 9:57). *Just tell me what You want me to do.* To which Jesus replied, indirectly, "Foxes have dens, and birds of the sky have nests, but the Son of Man has no place to lay His head" (v. 58). Be expected, in other words, not to know where your next meal is coming from. Can you be good with that?

"First let me go bury my father," said another (v. 59), which didn't really mean his dad was dead, but more likely that he'd be catching up with Jesus after a while. "I will follow You, Lord, but first let me go and say good-bye to those at my house" (v. 61)—again, a dodge for time and further deliberation.

Follow Me. That's what Jesus said to the people He was calling into service. Just "follow Me"—plain and simple—and I'll lead you to the place I've decided for you to go. Discipleship didn't come with a list of available menu options, in a range of styles and colors, suited to fit someone's schedule, complete with custom packages that offered upgrades in possible living conditions. Here's what they could expect—and here's what *we* can expect—"If anyone wants to come with Me, he must deny himself, take up his cross daily, and follow Me."

Now we've seen that our God is good. He loves us. He wants what's best for us. "I know the plans I have for you," He said to the Jewish exiles, "plans for your welfare, not for disaster, to give you a future and a hope" (Jer. 29:11). He's not intent on making our lives as austere and distasteful as He can possibly make them. He's not one of those, you know, who says, *You'll eat it, and you're going to like it.* That's not at all the heart behind this.

But the expectations you've brought into marriage— what if those aren't your reality? What if His plans for your marriage and family involve something else entirely— something *different*, yet something that could prove even *better* than what you've always had in mind . . . if you'll accept it with contentment, with optimism, even with joy?

To say that marriage is a unique relationship among all others is a legitimately general statement of fact. But no less true is the fact that *your* marriage—the union of the one-of-a-kind you with the one-of-a-kind him or her—is unique from all other marriages, past or present. The designs that God has set apart for your specific pairing are not exact duplicates of what He's done and is doing with others you know.

Your marriage may borrow certain things from the successful model of others, but it still needs its own experiences and identity, because your marriage is unique in a thousand ways. And if you'll just follow Him, He can make it so much better than any old personal preferences of yours could ever do.

Day 4

The Same, Only Different

Uniqueness Is Good

God has placed each one of the parts in one body just as He wanted. And if they were all the same part, where would the body be? (1 Corinthians 12:18–19)

If only he wasn't so . . .

It only she wasn't so . . .

What, you want them to be different? By being the same as you? On the same page? Same wavelength? Same opinion? Same way of looking at things?

That would be great, of course, if you were trying to be yardsticks. Or one-gallon milk cartons. Or those little six-sided oyster crackers people put on top of their tomato soup. Being identical twins would be a real plus for you then. You'd be better off, in fact, from being so uniform. Being different in that case would create some problems for you.

But you're a couple. You're married. You were even *attracted* to each other by some of these differences. You liked the way he was spontaneous when you were so tightly planned and budgeted. You liked how she made such comfortable conversation, since you tended to feel sort of shy and awkward in unstructured social settings. Sure, you loved the traits and interests you *shared*, too, but what sold you on this person was the whole package. They were *you*, but they were *themselves*, too, and they were . . .

They're *yours* now.

And you're not so sure being different is such a good thing.

Paul the apostle ran across a group of people who apparently were struggling hard with this matter of diversity. The church in Corinth, like too many churches today, wasn't getting along with each other very well—for lots of reasons, obviously, but many of their issues orbited around their differences. Like their difference in spiritual gifts, for example. Some of them were gifted in specific areas; others were gifted somewhere else. And while this combination of strengths could've come together under God's leadership into a vibrant, versatile powerhouse of worship and ministry opportunities, the church instead had descended into a bickering bunch of same-team enemies.

We can imagine how it was actually playing out. If someone excelled in a gifting area that put them more up front, made them more vocal, drew more attention to themselves—they could be talked about behind their back by those whose own abilities kept them relegated to, say, the baby nursery or the boiler room. I mean, who wants to be part of the invisible ordinary when some guy who's no more special than us is hogging all the big-Christian accolades and getting to sing the choir solos? Part of this problem, naturally, was fueled by people who really *did* think they were a touch more special because of the things they were capable of doing in the church. And they probably didn't mind if you got the clear message that you and your job didn't quite measure up to theirs in terms of importance.

Paul jumped right into the middle of this situation. "There are different gifts," he said, stating what should've been obvious to anyone, "but the same Spirit. There are different ministries, but the same Lord" (1 Cor. 12:4–5)—"many parts, yet one body" (v. 20). They unite us into a single organism that's stronger because of its individual components.

Our marriages are intended to be much the same. "If the whole body were an eye, where would the hearing be? If the whole body were an ear, where would the sense of smell be? But now God has placed each one of the parts in one body just as He wanted. And if they were all the same part, where would the body be?" (vv. 17–19).

Our differences from each other are certainly potential flashpoints of friction and disharmony. Whenever we feel pressured by our spouse's opposing sense of perspective or their unusual way (to us) of solving a problem and handling a crisis, we can feel like banging our head against the doorjamb. We just don't get it. *How can you possibly believe a plan like that will work? What do you not see about what I'm saying? Why won't you stop and think before you do something like that? You're driving me CRAZY here!*

But we actually *need* these differences that each of us brings to the table. They need your more cautious side; you need their more daring side. They need your sense of calmness to settle them down; you need their high energy to bring you out of yourself a little. They need your quick generosity so they don't become overly fixated on protecting and nearly hoarding your shared assets; yet you need their wise discernment so you're not quite as gullible and easily taken advantage of.

Otherwise, the sameness—though making you strong in specific areas—can make you extraordinarily weak in others, those places where neither of you possesses a chromosome for that particular character trait. When that happens, both of you are late everywhere you go; both of you are indecisive, paralyzed by anxiety and second-guessing; both of you are useless at being able to take a paint swatch and imagine how the whole room will look in that color.

But by allowing these tendencies and temperaments enough space to work together, surrounding them with an appreciative, respectful attitude of acceptance and compromise, you guys could make a really solid pair . . . by keeping your differences attractive to each other.

Day 5

Can I Trust You?

Loyalty and Reliability

*A good name is to be chosen over great wealth; favor
is better than silver and gold. (Proverbs 22:1)*

Coming into marriage, you arrive with a number of extremely valuable treasures in your possession. But none is more valuable perhaps than your *trustworthiness*, and it must be guarded with the utmost care. For if you lose it, you may just lose all the rest put together.

That's a hard statement to read. Hard statement to write. But ask any wife or husband who's lost the trust of his or her spouse—whether as the one who's broken trust themselves, or the one whose trust has been broken—and you'll discover a whole new definition of what the word *hard* truly means.

Marriage, we learn as we go along, comes with all kinds of outside influences and challenges that work against the life we're trying to build together. Demands from our jobs and other commitments can consistently ask for more of our time than we should probably give them—at least not week after week, again and again. Storm damage can wipe out a fencerow in the backyard, costing several hundred hard-earned dollars to clean up, repair, and haul away. Cars can break down; kids can get sick; bills can pile up; in-laws can be intrusive. There's enough stuff out there trying to create trouble for us that if all we did all day long was to fend it off and manage it as best we know how, our hands would be plenty full already.

But when we add to this long list of incoming struggles the drain of our own in-house turmoil, that's when marriage becomes too much to handle sometimes. If we can't be sure that our wife or husband is telling us everything that's going on . . . if we're hiding something from our mate that we don't want them to see or know about . . . if we're less than confident that some of the things we discuss and reveal about ourselves in private conversation won't end up being shared among others without our permission, or might be used against us as a verbal weapon at some point of marital tension down the road . . .

When trust is strained, *everything* is strained.

Think of it. Among the many reasons for why we enjoy such strength, courage, and comfort as a believer in Christ, one of the lesser visible ones is that we never need to worry whether we can trust Him or not. It goes without saying. Sure, we may not understand all His ways. We may get impatient sometimes with His silences. We may not know why He hasn't prevented a tough ordeal from happening to us. But name one thing He's ever done that puts His trustworthiness under suspicion. And good luck trying to defend your answer.

"The word of the LORD is right, and all His work is trustworthy" (Ps. 33:4). "God is not a man who lies, or a son of man who changes His mind. Does He speak and not act, or promise and not fulfill?" (Num. 23:19). Of course not. We trust Him. Implicitly. As David said, "Our fathers trusted in You; they trusted, and You rescued them. They cried to You and were set free; they trusted in You and were not disgraced" (Ps. 22:4–5)—because He always proves Himself trustworthy. Always has. We'd be sunk if He wasn't.

Relationships of all types require trust as a building block. Business relationships, friendships, relationships between neighbors. But no other relationship besides marriage, of course, is so close, so vulnerable. No other relationship is dependent on being able to trust this one other person with every aspect of our lives—our hopes, our memories, our hurts, our everything. And if I can't trust you . . . if you can't trust me . . . if we don't work hard at building a consistent track record of both candidness and competence . . . we're going nowhere fast toward anywhere good.

Trust and *truth* come from the same general root word. Both terms speak of faithfulness, of reliability. But *truth*, we know, is not merely a technical term, one that we narrowly define or consider complete by its bare bones alone. You can generally tell the truth, you know, without actually telling the truth—what you did, what you didn't do, what you said, what you didn't say, what you spent, what it actually cost, what you committed yourself to taking on, what it's really going to mean.

So in matters of *trust*, as in matters of *truth*, more is usually better. Details are preferable to rough outlines. Describing your thought process may be as important to your wife or husband as the action itself. Oversimplification is fine as a quick conveyor of information, but if asked to expand later, be prepared to explain in greater depth, without getting all dodgy, accusatory, defensive, or resistant.

Solomon wisely counseled his children to "guard your heart above all else, for it is the source of life. Don't let your mouth speak dishonestly, and don't let your lips talk deviously" (Prov. 4:23–24). Instead, "carefully consider the path for your feet, and all your ways will be established," not turning "to the right or to the left," but walking in open, well-lit, well-trodden spaces (vv. 26–27).

And since trust is one of those things that lives at the "heart" of your marriage, *guard it well* by avoiding any step that causes your spouse to wonder if you're being totally transparent.

"Many a man proclaims his own loyalty," the Bible says, "but who can find a trustworthy man?" (Prov. 20:6). If your spouse finds one of those rare men or women in you, they have found a treasure indeed.

Day 6

Big Fan

Being an Encourager

*I have great joy and encouragement from
your love, because the hearts of the saints have
been refreshed through you. (Philemon 7)*

We're still a ways off from the place in this book when we're going to be talking specifically about the "submission" thing—which some biblical critics decry as the one-and-only, sum total of everything God says on the subject of marriage. But maybe this hot-button issue wouldn't burn through *anyone's* sensitivities so quickly if we pulled back the lens a bit so we could see this important concept in all its colors and context . . . in a factual light that all of us should find entirely reasonable.

Like, who'd be opposed, for example, to the idea of both of us just being on the same side? Wanting to help? Being each other's biggest fans?

After all, potential icy patches like submission don't really become much of an issue anyway until we're unable to see eye to eye on something, until we've created a scenario in which one of us needs to make a decision on a matter or else we'll be stuck in this state of limbo forever. And while these conflicts are sure to surface from time to time in marriage, maybe we could cut back on their sheer volume simply by making a habit of being more *encouraging* of one another—husband to wife, wife to husband. Maybe some of the disagreements we've allowed to morph into much bigger deals—maybe they'd rarely reach such a level of intensity if we were more devoted to maintaining a deliberate posture of support toward what our spouse is doing, thinking, dreaming, and desiring.

Encouragement. What makes us withhold it? What makes us so stingy with it sometimes? Why might a friend or coworker perhaps be more likely to enjoy the benefit of our enthusiasm and cheerleading than our own wife or husband? Why might we catch ourselves only half listening to our spouse's ideas and suggestions, rolling our eyes in a here-they-go-again shutdown of interest in what they're wanting or proposing? Is it because we want to retain the told-you-so option? In case their thinking proves off base later on or comes up short of their expectations?

Could be. Jesus hit on the truism that "a prophet is not without honor except in his hometown and in his household" (Matt. 13:57). Familiarity with our mate's propensity for getting all gung-ho about a new project, then fizzling out in the follow-through, may cause us to draw back from being overly vocal in our support. We may think we're actually doing them a favor by discouraging them from this direction, by pointing out the red flags they're obviously not wanting to see and consider.

But even in legitimately trying to keep their feet on the ground, we should ask ourselves: Are we turning into such an automatic no in their head that eventually they'll just learn not to bother coming to us at all with their plans—for making money, making changes, or whatever—figuring their ideas will just get shot down anyway?

Paul the apostle was a big proponent of encouragement. Once a notorious persecutor of Christians, he himself wasn't immediately popular as a candidate for hanging around with church people. He might not have been welcomed into the warmth of their fellowship at all if not for the commendable endorsement of Barnabas (Acts 9:26–27), a man whose name meant "Son of Encouragement" (4:36). Paul also, because of his frequent stays in prison and other places of confinement, loved getting an encouraging word from the churches he'd helped to establish (Phil. 2:19), and often sent an associate to go visit them in his absence, "to let you know how we are and to encourage your hearts" (Eph. 6:22). Part of his desire for wanting to finally make it to Rome and meet the members of the church there was "to be mutually encouraged by each other's faith, both yours and mine" (Rom. 1:12).

Many of the admonitions that come down to us through Paul's letters tell us to "encourage one another," to "build each other up" as we go along (1 Thess. 5:11). Granted, sometimes his purpose for telling them to give encouragement carried a kick-in-the-pants aspect to it—*that* kind of "encouragement," you know. But the end result was to make sure believers were getting behind one another, urging their brothers and sisters forward in living for Christ.

Your spouse, if they're like most people, performs better when they're receiving your encouraging support, rather than when they're constantly enduring the headwinds of your contrary opinion—or even just your measured doubts, which you want to be sure you've gone on record as saying. Again, this doesn't mean blindly agreeing with them—*whatever you say, dear*—nodding behind vacuous eyes, ever the silent partner, knowing not to cross what they've determined to do.

All opinions should be welcome in marriage. Healthy debate and dialogue make good ideas better. No one should be deemed a downer simply for asking good, probing questions.

But how many times in your marriage do you say (and hopefully hear) the words, "I just want you to know I'm proud of you." "You're so good at that." "Okay, let's try it, if you feel like that's the thing to do." "I really appreciate how hard you've been working on this." "I believe in you—you can do it." "I think you're wonderful." "You're the best."

No, *you're* the best.

When you're being an encourager.

Day 7

Grounds for Forgiveness

Refusing to Be Offended

If he sins against you seven times in a day,
and comes back to you seven times, saying,
"I repent," you must forgive him. (Luke 17:4)

Few, if any, standard athletic skills are more difficult to develop than hitting a major league fastball. The science alone renders it nearly impossible. The amount of time that a batter is given for deciding whether or not to swing at a blazing 90–95-miles-per-hour pitch—it's a factor of milliseconds. Literally less than the blink of an eye. It's why Yogi Berra was famously quoted as saying, "You can't think and hit at the same time." The facts would tell you it just can't be done.

All this to say—when you see a pro baseball player on television swing and hit a pitch, even if he grounds into a double play or sends a lazy pop-up into left field, you are witnessing a miracle. Because if you or I were in the batter's box, we wouldn't even *see* the ball. It would already have zoomed past us and be on its way back to the pitcher. We wouldn't so much as tip it, not in a hundred tries. A hundred strike outs.

How does anyone do it then? How do they hit it? They do it by learning to hit the ball as second graders on a coach-pitch community team. By hitting balls from a twelve-year-old bruiser from across town in Little League. By hitting balls from competition in high school and college and the minor leagues, till they finally get that call-up to the majors. And even then, every day at the ballpark starts with what? Batting practice.

You work your way up. You learn as you go. You keep getting better at it all the time. Then when that day comes, and you're asked to step up to the plate . . . look at you. You're doing what everyone says is impossible.

That's what forgiveness is like.

When we think about forgiveness—why it's so hard, why it's such a struggle, why we could never see ourselves being able to forgive something as major-league as that (whatever *that* is)—we often go straight to the most extreme examples. Not necessarily adultery, which seems to come first to mind. But whatever the case, we think of those particular betrayals or borderline abuses that touch us at our deepest places— especially when coming from this one person who's supposed to love us and protect us like no other. *I'll never—I could never—forgive them for that.*

Absolutely, these kinds of blows can be painfully difficult to forgive and move beyond. We are right in surmising, even with the heroic infusion of our forgiveness, that the fallout and rebuilding of trust will take some time. We've been hurt. Healing is a process.

But the ability to forgive even *that* offense comes largely from building a heart of instant forgiveness over the long term, when the offenses are as simple as misplacing the keys, dinging the car door, staining our favorite shirt, or forgetting to turn on the Crock-Pot for Sunday lunch. When our first response toward our wife's or husband's mistakes is to forgive—"it's okay, sweetie, don't worry about it"—we increase the spiritual hand-eye coordination that makes us able to fight for peace even when an issue becomes more serious.

The jaded among us would say, "Wait, we're just giving them permission to walk all over us. If they know we're such an easy touch, they'll never stop to consider what their actions against us could cost them."

But actually, we're just giving them the kind of grace we've been given as recipients of God's mercy. Do you consider His forgiveness of you to be permission to do whatever you want without consequence? Forgiving our spouse may mean we'll be hurt again, sure—just as our sins "grieve" the Spirit of God every time (Eph. 4:30). But God's forgiveness is actually what keeps us coming back to our senses as redeemed sinners, back to the love that leads us where we truly want to go. "God's kindness is intended to lead you to repentance" (Rom. 2:4).

So use your forgiveness to lead your wife or husband to that place as well. *To real repentance.*

Your anger, after all, will most likely only drive them away, widening the distance that their sin or negligence has already caused. Sin can always be counted on to contaminate a marriage—their sin, your sin. But forgiveness is what keeps your relationship cleaned out and fluid, able to run smoothly again. It may be messy at first. May not seem to be working. But every other alternative will result in added breakdown, blockage, dead ends, and ultimately despair.

Jesus was right, of course—*repentance* on your spouse's part is a key ingredient in making your forgiveness successful. If they don't care, if they don't think they did anything wrong, if they say you're the one who's actually more to blame, the only thing your forgiveness can do, really, is help you stay in a place of contented, God-trusting freedom yourself while He personally deals with them and their issues. But "just as the Lord has forgiven you, so you must also forgive" (Col. 3:13). And since we know how often we hit the "seven times a day" mark in our own lives, only to be forgiven by Him again and again, maybe we shouldn't consider it such an unbearable intrusion when we're the ones being sinned against.

Jesus called it a "must." Calling them forgiven.

You never know: another opportunity may be coming down the pike today, a chance to practice the kind of gracious love that keeps marriages from turning into bitter rivalries. So if your wife or husband comes to you asking forgiveness— plant your feet, take your best cut, and see if you can't just hit this one out of the park.

Day 8

My Time Is Your Time
Prioritizing Each Other

There is an occasion for everything, and a time for
every activity under heaven. (Ecclesiastes 3:1)

There is time to do everything God has given you to
do today.

This stark assessment may sound naïvely ridiculous
to you as you read it. Because even with doing your dead-level
best, even with shoehorning everybody's expectations into
the cramped quarters of each twenty-four hours, perhaps
you rarely close out a day without feeling woefully behind.
The mail is still unopened on the desk or filing cabinet.
The laundry stacks are pouring out into the hallway. You're
nowhere near as prepared as you'd like to be for the session or
meeting you're leading tomorrow. And—oh, man, this kitchen

drawer that keeps sticking whenever you open it? When are you ever getting around to fixing that?

We know it, right? We feel your pain.

But though Jesus first spoke the following phrase in what we'd call a much simpler time, His Word is eternal enough to carry over into the affairs of every generation, including ours. "Give us each day our daily bread," He said, in teaching His disciples to pray (Luke 11:3). This familiar line from the Lord's Prayer may sound spiritually sentimental at church service on a Sunday morning, but it's actually meant to frame up a divine promise that is ours to claim every day for as long as we live. And unless our marriages orbit around this nucleus of trust in God's provision—and of peace in His perspective— we will always be meeting ourselves coming and going, and we'll miss out on meeting the needs in each other that make our marriage what He intended it to be.

"Each day." The Bible often counsels us to keep our attention focused on today. "Don't worry about tomorrow," Jesus said, "because tomorrow will worry about itself. Each day has enough trouble of its own" (Matt. 6:34). A lot of the reason why we struggle to stay fully engaged in the moment, why we're not sure we can afford to spend much time together as a couple, is because we're haunted by what we're *not* doing while we're doing what we're *currently* doing. We're concerned that just quieting down here for a little while, making ourselves unbusy for one another, will cost us too much later, that we'll end up paying for it tomorrow.

Now, obviously we've got responsibilities. We have lots of things to accomplish and to be working on. But often we're as defined by what we choose to delay and put off as by what we choose to invest in. If today (as most days do) needs to include a stretch of time where we do nothing but talk and take care of each other, we must ruggedly decide to give our full selves to these moments without letting tomorrow impinge on them and steal what's right here, right now, to experience.

"Daily bread." Like the manna that God provided the ancient Israelites in the wilderness, He continues to give us a full supply of what we need for managing the matters of each day. The people of that generation in Bible history probably had days when they might've liked a little more manna to go around. They might've doubted sometimes if they could slice and dice it enough different ways to make it stretch through the evening. Yet it was always enough. And it was always there the next morning, ready to provide the needed nutrients for the day, even without holding over any extra from the day before.

This "daily bread" that Jesus has promised us may not be enough to cover everything we *want* to do. Neither will it be enough to give every child, every client, and every chore—all of them—our round-the-clock attention, as if whatever they demand must automatically be accomplished, no matter how it affects everybody else. But though this "daily bread" must be allocated onto all your various plates, God has already gone ahead of you to decide what you're meant to handle. So with a combination of prayer, hard work, and wise decisions—as well as a judicious use of the word *no* as an acceptable answer to certain requests—you can now proceed with confidence, knowing there's enough of you to go around when "you serve the Lord Christ" (Col. 3:24).

And if your handling of the day pleases *Him*, all these days will add up into a lifetime of doing the right things—the best things—all along.

Life is comprised of different seasons. That's what the writer of Ecclesiastes was trying to say in the poetic stretch of opening verses from chapter 3 of his book: "A time to weep and a time to laugh; a time to mourn and a time to dance; a time to throw stones and a time to gather stones; a time to embrace and a time to avoid embracing" (vv. 4–5). Not every day will look like the next. Depending on the kind of work you do or the stage of life you're currently living, you will go through periods when you'll need to press more heavily into one area or another. Your spouse will need to understand you'll be tied up and preoccupied more than usual.

But the cultivation of your marriage must remain a priority. Other things can't knock your wife or husband off your schedule all the time. They need to know that although your job, your friends, your church obligations, and other such things are each important and necessary parts of your life, no day would ever be the same in your eyes if they weren't a major part of it.

You're certainly tasked with making choices—sometimes *hard* choices—on how you'll spend your time. But time with *them* is something you must never be willing to compromise. Because when God makes His plans for what should go on your calendar, you can bet they're an A-lister.

Even if somebody else needs to wait their turn.

Day 9

Dollar Amounts
Handling Your Money

Those who want to be rich fall into temptation, a trap, and many foolish and harmful desires, which plunge people into ruin and destruction. (1 Timothy 6:9)

They say that money is one of the most frequent topics of conversation in our homes as married couples—and among the most common sources of disagreement that we face.

Should we buy the newer car with the lower miles and extended warranty? Or should we instead take the much cheaper one that hopefully won't need too many repairs?

Should we fork out the big bucks for private school education? Or should we instead consider putting the kids in public school and investing more of our money for college?

Should we increase our retirement fund allocations to match what they say is on track for our future goals? Or should we instead take slightly more of a live-now approach?

We could fill up this whole page with likely scenarios—places where our general financial philosophy can color a wide variety of ongoing discussions and decisions. And while neither one of us needs to completely sell out to how the other one thinks and believes in such matters, we do need to make sure that we're aligning ourselves (both of us) with what the Bible clearly teaches as wise, obedient money management. Otherwise, we're in for some relational imbalances we'll never be able to reconcile.

Here's what we might consider the high spots:

Giving. Many people think the only financial guidance we find in the Bible is the part about how we're supposed to be more generous, less stingy and miserly. And though it actually tells us a lot more than that, the Word does teach us to "give to the one who asks you, and don't turn away from the one who wants to borrow from you" (Matt. 5:42) . . . to "do what is good and lend, expecting nothing in return. Then your reward will be great, and you will be sons of the Most High" (Luke 6:35).

The standard amount that God instructed His people to give to Him as an act of worship was always the tithe—meaning, a tenth—dating all the way back to the days of Abraham (Gen. 14:20), Jacob (28:22), Moses (Lev. 27:30), everybody. Perhaps the most explicit passage that echoes this expectation is found in Malachi 3, where God challenged His people to "bring the full tenth into the storehouse so that there may be food in My house." In fact, "test Me in this way," He said, and "see if I will not open the floodgates of heaven and pour out a blessing for you without measure" (v. 10).

Jesus didn't specify a certain giving amount or percentage, although His teachings always carried the expectation that we should do more than keep just the bare minimums of the law (Matt. 5:20). Paul told the New Testament believers to enjoy the freedom of not giving "reluctantly or out of necessity" but to become instead "a cheerful giver," confident that God will provide "everything you need" so that you can "excel in every good work" (2 Cor. 9:7–8).

Bottom line: you can't out give God; you'll be richer in many ways from being more generous; and those who maintain an open, caring heart for the poor and needy are some of the happiest, most Christlike people in the world. Don't you want your marriage to be a place that routinely experiences those kinds of blessings?

Greed. Solomon observed that "the one who loves money is never satisfied with money" (Eccles. 5:10), that "as soon as your eyes fly to it, it disappears, for it makes wings for itself and flies like an eagle to the sky" (Prov. 23:5). Jesus warned people to "watch out and be on guard against all greed because one's life is not in the abundance of his possessions" (Luke 12:15). And Paul instructed the young pastor Timothy to tell his congregation "not to be arrogant or to set their hope on the uncertainty of wealth, but on God, who richly provides us all things to enjoy" (1 Tim. 6:17).

The contrasting character trait to greed, of course, is *contentment*—which, as it turns out, can be one of the sweetest gifts you ever give to each other. When the pressure of achieving a certain level of economic status is off the table, along with the distracting energy required of all its accumulated extras, you can spend more time simply enjoying one another's company, developing your outside relationships, becoming rich in experiences that will last a lifetime. Not fighting over money.

You'd think it wouldn't matter, really—talking out your sometimes unspoken views on financial usage and strategy. But it does. Agreeing about your savings goals and priorities. Sharing the commitment of staying out of debt. Accepting Jesus' challenge not to worry about whether He'll provide everything you need. These *will* become arguments (if they haven't already) if you simply wait for life to bring them up. They'll become one of the back doors your Enemy uses to try stealing your peace of mind and your unity of focus. They'll cost you things that don't even show up on credit card statements, sales receipts, and tax returns.

But you and your mate can take a deliberate step toward avoiding or defusing these ticking time bombs, areas where anxiety and squabbles over money are capable of taking you away from the main business of marriage. By submitting to God's Word and seeking common ground, you'll receive the kinds of dividends that'll keep you feeling secure and satisfied with each other year after year.

Bank on it.

Day 10

Marriage's Message
The Gospel in Miniature

This mystery is profound, but I am talking about
Christ and the church. (Ephesians 5:32)

Marriage is not just what people do when they grow up. It's not merely the expected next step for a couple who's met and been dating and are starting to get serious. Marriage comes with a long, long history. And an enormous level of importance, beyond just its significance to the two of you and your families. By entering into it, you've not only pledged your heart to your lifelong love. You've also been handed stewardship over a treasure that could be your greatest single tool for making a kingdom impact in your world, or else the one thing that dilutes or invalidates your Christian testimony more than any other demographic that identifies you.

Marriage is a living picture of the gospel.

The proof of marriage's gravitas can be seen by how early it makes an appearance on the scene of creation history. No sooner than the second chapter of Genesis, before the earth was populated by more than one human—the *first* human—God was already planning a wedding. "It is not good for the man to be alone," the Lord said. "I will make a helper as his complement" (Gen. 2:18). No other readily available being was deemed suitable to such a task. Only God's special creation of woman would do. And by the end of chapter 2, with Eden still in its state of pure perfection, the first man and first woman had become the first husband and wife.

So we're talking *important*. One of God's highest, first-thing priorities. At a time when He was setting up the kinds of arrangements and order that would reflect His divine purposes for life on this planet, the institution of marriage was among His primary objectives.

He knew, of course, that trouble was brewing. He knew before time began that Adam's descendants—aka "all of us"—would inherit a sin nature that would prevent us from experiencing fellowship with a holy God. He knew we would be totally dependent on Christ, our atoning Substitute, in order to be received before His throne with righteous standing. We would need to be sought and found and loved into His arms, and then submit ourselves to Him as the One to whom we owe our total allegiance.

Marriage—as He knew—would become a universally understood relationship, one that would provide a protective cocoon for a man and wife to experience intimacy with one another, as well as to establish their own homes and families. But it would also be a portrait of Christ's relationship with the church. And in Ephesians 5, we get the whole thing spelled out for us—a powerful mixture of practical instruction and spiritual mystery.

Marriage is to be a covenant of unconditional, unbreakable love, the way Christ has promised Himself to us, the way He has loved His church—His people—at the cost of His own life. He "gave Himself for her to make her holy, cleansing her with the washing of water by the word. He did this to present the church to Himself in splendor, without spot or wrinkle" (Eph. 5:25–27).

So *that's* why husbands are supposed to "love their wives as their own bodies" (v. 28). They've been *called* to it. They don't just provide and care for their wives because that's what good men do or because this woman is their one-and-only sweetheart. All of that is *true* hopefully, and vitally important, yet it's spiritually and eternally secondary.

God's overarching, number one reason for a man to love his wife with kill-me-dead loyalty is so that people who know them and recognize them can say, "See how he loves her? That's how Jesus loves us."

Wow.

You think that doesn't drive up the responsibility for why keeping our marriage vows is so crucial and inviolable? We're not just being true to each other; the quality of our relationship is meant to point to a much, much greater truth.

That's why when Christian marriages fail or become cross and contentious, they don't merely become sources of personal unhappiness; they forfeit their chief purpose. A husband who doesn't both fiercely and tenderly love his wife can't really speak to his kids with much authority and connection about the difference Jesus makes in his life. A wife who doesn't respect and honor her husband creates a real hurdle to overcome if she wants to be a winsome example to her friends and neighbors of what a relationship with Christ is like.

This is not just setting up housekeeping.

Your marriage is meant to send a message.

It's fascinating to wonder sometimes why God has chosen to organize and color His creation the way He's done. Why up is up. Why purple is pretty. Why one seed in the ground produces such a multiple of new seeds for regrowth. The laws and properties of nature were His own to design, and He fashioned them all with infinite intentionality. Creation is not just "the way it is." It's the way He wanted it.

So marriage, like the change of seasons, is not just a normal, desirable rite of passage. Marriage, like all these other things, is a deliberate God invention. And while He is creative and loving enough to let it serve for us a number of different reasons, He made it for one special reason—to show forth His glory.

And you get to do that too. Just by living out your marriage.

Day 11

Honor Thy Parents

Balancing Family

*Honor your father and mother, which is the
first commandment with a promise, so that it
may go well with you and that you may have
a long life in the land. (Ephesians 6:2–3)*

I n the 1950s-era television game show *Beat the Clock*,
contestants were asked to complete an assigned task of
dexterity and skill within sixty seconds, while the time
wound down on a huge clock in the center of the studio. The
stunts themselves were often fairly simple in theory—stack
a certain number of plates, move a group of boxes from one
part of the stage to the other, fill up six helium balloons. But
just before starting the clock on a player's challenge, the host
would then introduce a difficulty or obstacle into the mix.
Like, maybe the person would need to do it blindfolded, or

with someone sitting on their shoulders, or without being able to use their hands. Suddenly a straightforward undertaking became well-nigh impossible.

They could do the *one* thing if it weren't for the *other* thing.

Perhaps the most basic, foundational statement made about marriage in Scripture is found immediately after God created Eve, using a rib taken from Adam's side, making her "bone of my bone and flesh of my flesh" (Gen. 2:23). As the Genesis narrative goes on to explain, "This is why a man leaves his father and mother and bonds with his wife, and they become one flesh" (v. 24). Jesus repeated the same verse when questioned by the Pharisees about His interpretation of divorce law (Matt. 19:5). Paul quoted a piece of it in clarifying the basis for sexual purity, as well as the corresponding sinfulness of sexual immorality (1 Cor. 6:16).

A man, a woman—they leave their homes of origin to establish a new home for themselves. They "leave and cleave," as we often say in summarizing this biblical imperative of marriage.

Okay. We can *do* that. Not a problem.

But then . . .

No lesser authority than the Ten Commandments comes along with this feature as Rule #5: "Honor your father and your mother so that you may have a long life in the land that the Lord your God is giving you" (Exod. 20:12). Obey them. Esteem them. Respect them. Care for them. We owe them by God's command a lifetime of love and allegiance for bearing us and shepherding us from our earliest days all throughout our childhood and adolescence.

Now, obviously these two directives—(1) leaving our parents; (2) honoring our parents—can both be done without trampling on the other. In theory. But at the same time, they do present some challenging conflicts that can threaten to make observing one of these commands nearly impossible while still upholding the other. In practice.

It's going to be a balancing act.

Part of the problem, of course, can be on *our* end. Depending on how strong or passive our drive toward independence has been, the "leaving home" aspect of marriage may or may not have proven too difficult for us. Some newlyweds can't wait to pull away; others still can hardly imagine a Sunday lunch without mama's roast beef and homemade biscuits in it. The pull of the familiar. The nostalgic homesickness for an earlier time, a place where everything just felt more nailed down and secure. Safe. It can keep drawing us back. At the expense of establishing a new, strong, developing home with our spouse.

However, part of the problem can arise from moms and/or dads who don't make this healthy severing of ties an easy thing for a couple to accomplish. Guilt trips, manipulation, control tactics, sentimental appeals for attention, not wanting to share their little boy or girl (and certainly not their little grandkids) with another set of competing parents.

So there can be tension here. A split-in-half sense of loyalty. And in those moments where the situation seems (whether it actually does or not) to be calling for a deliberate, gotta-pick-one choice between one or the other . . . that's where the challenge comes in.

You alone know all the personalized dynamics that press against this potentially fragile dichotomy in your own life.

Maybe, thankfully, it's not much of an issue in your marriage at all. You guys have figured it out and are sailing through the middle ground with relative ease. Perhaps, though, struggles over this central topic are at the volcanic source of most of your disagreements and misunderstandings. And if you could only land on a livable solution that made this balance navigable, you'd be almost excited about moving on to a new problem to deal with. Anything but this.

The truth, of course, is that your first allegiance—each of you—is to God, who has given both of these commands to you as a means toward bringing blessing into your life. You please Him every time you choose one-flesh unity and devotion with each other, allowing Him to make of your home an all-new outpost for His name to be honored and His work to be done. You please Him, too, when your heart is genuinely devoted toward honoring your parents, whether they've been honorable toward you throughout their lives or not. Your job is not to meet every request and expectation they might make on you. But your service toward them, especially as they enter their later years and may require additional types of physical care, is an offering of gratitude both to them and to Him.

It'll require some finesse from time to time, as you likely know. But nothing can keep you from being true to both obligations in God's eyes—your now superior loyalty to your spouse, as well as your appropriate expressions of honor toward your parents. And, yes, your in-laws.

Stay seeking Him. He'll show you what to do.

Day 12

Wisely Done
Moving toward Maturity

*A house is built by wisdom, and it is
established by understanding; by knowledge
the rooms are filled with every precious and
beautiful treasure. (Proverbs 24:3–4)*

Life is too big for us.

The weird thing, the tricky thing, is that it doesn't always seem this way. We can be going along, getting into a pretty good routine—the gym at 6:00, work by 8:30, a sandwich and soft drink brought from home for lunch, Wednesday-night church, friends over on Friday. Feels like we've got everything right where we want it. Mostly smiles and hugs and "love you, babe," a peck on the cheek as we peel out into another day.

But ask anybody. *An-y-body.* And they'll tell you. The day is coming. The shoe will drop. Something will approach in your blind spot. Maybe three things all at once. The consequence of a sin you've been trying to manage but haven't exactly been totally eradicating. The general trajectory of decay that exists in your car engine and household appliances and other weight-bearing possessions in your life. The failures of others around you that you and your spouse were counting on for stability, or at least not to become a time-consuming problem. Hiccups in your health, frustrations with your noisy neighbors, downturns in the economy or in your own specific industry.

It might be the result of "your adversary the Devil," who is always "prowling around like a roaring lion, looking for anyone he can devour" (1 Pet. 5:8). Or it might be God acting in your life as "a refiner and purifier of silver" (Mal. 3:3), using certain situations and circumstances to purify and grow you and strengthen you for what He knows is coming. It might even be a stretch of successes, people singing your praises—pride-inducing moments that can sometimes harbor the most potential danger of all, since hardships more naturally drive us to our knees in humble prayer and dependence (Prov. 27:21).

But whatever comes, whenever it happens, you and your marriage won't be big and tough enough to handle it. Not without wisdom.

We all need all the wisdom we can get.

And today is the right day to get it.

"Get wisdom, get understanding; don't forget or turn away from the words of my mouth," said Solomon to his children, hoping they'd listen where most decide they already know better (Prov. 4:5). "Don't abandon wisdom, and she will watch over you; love her, and she will guard you. Wisdom is supreme—so get wisdom. And whatever else you get, get understanding. Cherish her, and she will exalt you; if you embrace her, she will honor you. She will place a garland of grace on your head; she will give you a crown of beauty" (vv. 6–9).

Sounds like the passionate appeal of the same man—arguably the wisest man of all time—who would later write the mostly depressing, downcast, regret-laden book of Ecclesiastes. That's where he reflected back on missed opportunities and misplaced priorities, exposing the largely unadvertised downsides of things like wealth and overwork and learning and pleasure seeking. Amazing that God would allow writing of this type to exist within His holy canon. Shows how honest and real is this life of faith—no plastic, pie-in-the-sky, out-of-reality bunch of foolishness. In fact, that's why He has put within our reach so much access to His wisdom and counsel—so we can approach the uncertainties of life with the time-proven certainty of His perspective.

So dig into His Word together. Both of you. As one. With others. By yourself. Ask questions of people who model the kind of life and marriage you want to shoot toward, whose everyday example shows all the signs of being marked by maturity and steadiness and exceptionally good sense. Be an acquirer of wisdom, same as other people seek to acquire whatever stuff or status they're so eagerly working for.

The book of Proverbs, you probably know, is the one place in the Bible where every verse is intended for this explicit purpose: the transference of wisdom. It's where we learn, among many other things . . .

- "The fear of the LORD is the beginning of knowledge" (Prov. 1:7).
- "A man's heart plans his way, but the LORD determines his steps" (16:9).
- "A gentle answer turns away anger, but a harsh word stirs up wrath" (15:1).
- "Better a dry crust with peace than a house full of feasting with strife" (17:1).
- "Wage war with sound guidance—victory comes with many counselors" (24:6).
- "Let another praise you, and not your own mouth—a stranger and not your own lips" (27:2).
- "The one who works his land will have plenty of food, but whoever chases fantasies lacks sense" (12:11).

Can't go wrong with that kind of advice.

So while life is out there waiting for you and your marriage, ready to run you over with its supersized challenges and unexpected interruptions—with its ever-ticking stopwatch and its ability to bite back at the worst possible moment—now is the time to build your house on wisdom. That's how you decorate all your rooms "with every precious and beautiful treasure"—form and function that never goes out of style.

Day 13

What Do You Want?

Goals and Dreams

May He give you what your heart desires and
fulfill your whole purpose. (Psalm 20:4)

Where do you want to go today?" It sounds so
archaic to hear it now, but in 1994, when
the world was just beginning to open up to
the Internet and to a revolutionary new way of accessing
entertainment and information, Microsoft's marketing slogan
intrigued users and viewers alike with a never-before-known
invitation to put the world at their fingertips.

Where do you want to go today?

Granted, there wasn't really much out there to see
yet. Not all that many places to go. Online encyclopedias.
Educational games. Slow dial-up. That creepy, screechy,

metallic connection sound, followed by "Hello! You've got mail." (I know, it's a world you probably wouldn't recognize.)

But "where do you want to go today?" millions were being asked to consider. Because maybe, just maybe, there was a way to get there.

How well would you say you know where your wife or husband is wanting to go? How well do you think they know where *you're* wanting to go? How often do you still talk about these things? Dream about them? Pray about them? Work together on them?

If you were guessing, do you think your spouse might be harboring any kind of hopes that, for one reason or another, they're too afraid to even bring up with you? Maybe because they'd think *you'd* think it was silly? Maybe because they don't have the confidence in themselves that they could ever actually pull it off? Maybe because they've decided to just give up on it? Without looking any further into it or investing any more thought or energy?

And you—do you have any of those yourself?

Perhaps it's not even anything huge. Or career-driven. Or permanently life altering. It's just that you always sort of wished you two could go on a cruise together. Or sign up for one of those mission trips your church sponsors every year. Or get your spouse interested in looking for bargain treasures with you at the flea market. You'd love doing that together.

You used to talk about things like this. Back when you were first getting to know one another. Back when everything you did and liked, when everything *they* did and liked, was such fascinating fodder for your imagination. But now you hardly ever mention it anymore, even though you sometimes catch yourself thinking about it. Wondering.

Oh well.

No—don't "oh well" it into oblivion already. Why can't you keep these goals and hopes alive—long enough to see if maybe they're also what God might have in mind for you, too, both individually and as a couple?

Life tends to settle. Tends to find its sofa cushions. Tends to roll together into weeks and months of just getting it done . . . as if getting it done is what it's all about.

Faith tends to settle too. Tends to round off its bold edges. Tends to become regular calendar appointments rather than true openings for our spirit to follow God wherever He leads us to go.

Marriage, of necessity, will always need to possess its rhythms and chores and everyday responsibilities. We must often be content with certain requirements and sameness and the occasional sense of boredom. But still, you and your spouse are the only ones in the position of deciding whether or not you're going to settle for putting your deepest desires to death, losing them underneath the pile of everyday life, just so you can keep treading water and staying afloat.

Because that's what happens to most people. They concede. They stop hoping. They lose the youthfulness and zeal that once drove them to dream. They forfeit through familiarity the quest for pulling out of their mate the things that most excite and inspire them. And while, yes, there can be mysteriously hidden beauty in the mundane details of life, just as there can be a peaceful acceptance of quietness in the process of growing older, the Scripture says God has put "eternity" in our hearts

(Eccles. 3:11). He has made us for more than just writing down our to-do lists and cutting up vegetables for supper. His Word tells us to "take delight in the LORD, and He will give you your heart's desires" (Ps. 37:4), to "commit your way to the LORD; trust in Him, and He will act, making your righteousness shine like the dawn, your justice like the noonday" (vv. 5–6).

So . . . what do you want? What kind of fire has He lit inside you that still sparks at regular intervals—not because of guilt, not because of jealousy, but simply because He's given you a passion for something that you haven't yet exercised the faith to pursue?

And what does your mate want? What would they love to see different by this time next year? What kinds of incremental steps would they like to take in the next six to nine months that would put fresh incentive and momentum behind one of their lifelong ambitions?

What could you do to make your home and marriage more of an open forum for expressing and exploring your goals? Keeping them front and center? Making them intentional, hand-holding matters of prayer? Plotting them on a map, working together to color them in and track your progress? Locating and listening for the right people who could partner with you in bringing this scattering of raw seeds to fruition?

You might be surprised at the conversation that would ensue if you'd sit down with each other and with your blue-sky list of wants and wishes.

It's sure not much of a surprise what'll happen if you don't.

Day 14

Deep Knee Bends
Praying Together

*I assure you: If two of you on earth agree on any
matter that you pray for, it will be done for you
by My Father in heaven. (Matthew 18:19)*

People are always looking for secrets—secrets to weight loss, secrets to a smoother complexion, secrets to putting more topspin on your backhand, secrets to keeping down the pet hair problem in the house. The secret to the last one is easy: either (a) don't let your pets inside, (b) don't let them climb around on the furniture, or (c) don't have pets. If none of these options appeal to you, you might just try vacuuming more often.

But probably the greatest secret to joy and longevity and togetherness in your *marriage* is really no secret at all.

Pray together.

Pray for each other.

Pray about everything.

Pray. Pray. Pray. Pray. Pray.

Paul instructed the people in one of the churches he helped establish to "pray constantly" (1 Thess. 5:17). We may not be sure how to do that and still hold down a steady job. But obviously, the meaning of his admonition was that prayer should be a running dialogue between ourselves and the Father, something we're continually coming in and out of, a daily stream of long talks and one-word paragraphs—praises of worship and appeals for strength. All day long. That's what prayer ought to be.

"Ought to be?" Those words, if God didn't understand us so well, would be deemed an insult. We *ought* to be communicating with Him? We *ought* to make time for Him in our busy little day? Listen, prayer is a gift. Prayer is not a human entitlement. God, after creating the world and setting it up to be generationally populated with people, could so easily have detached Himself from the whole thing and left us here to run it into the ground ourselves. He wasn't required to keep Himself available to us. He didn't need to establish a way for mortal man to personally correspond with Him. Yet He chose, by His loving grace, to promise us that we could call to Him and He would hear us, day or night, every single second of our lives.

Prayer is a blessing—beyond anything we should dare to claim or deserve—something that we can hardly believe has been included, for free, on our standard-issue tool belt. *Prayer.* Being able to talk with God. And hear from God. And even to wrap our arms around each other while we pray to Him together.

That's not something we *ought* to do.

Prayer is something we *get* to do.

So let's get to doing it.

But I don't know how. It's too awkward. I'm embarrassed. It feels so forced and unnatural. Yeah, and so does everything else until you start doing it. Won't take long, though, before nothing is more precious to you than the time you spend together, seeking His counsel, releasing your anxieties, thanking Him for the treasure of one another. Plus, you can know you'll be back here again, day after day, able to multiply your faith through the faith of your spouse, and know that the Lord is working out all your problems and issues "for the good of those who love God: those who are called according to His purpose" (Rom. 8:28).

That's a great place for the two of you to be.

Because God through prayer can do anything.

The feature verse from Matthew 18 that anchors this day's reading (verse 19—go back and reread it if you skipped over it) contains the words of Jesus, spoken in a very specific context. If you look at it in isolation from the rest of the passage, you might think Jesus is declaring His Father a genie who jumps at our magic wishes. The setting of the verse, however, is not just a general teaching topic, but rather a dispute between two fellow believers.

His instructions on how to handle this kind of problem suggests the seriousness of what the hypothetical offense could be—the kind that if not recognized and made right could result in the person being removed from church fellowship.

The goal of all the various steps He mentioned in verses 15–17—going to the person in private, then taking another person with you, before taking the matter before the entire congregation—is that "if he listens to you, you have won your brother" (v. 15). Seeking restoration and repentance and the healing of renewed relationship is what you're after, no matter how irreparable these cases may sometimes appear.

But "if two of you on earth agree" in prayer that God can do something this powerfully redemptive, even in that kind of dicey situation, "it will be done for you by My Father in heaven." He will hear your prayer; He knows your need; He knows what it takes; and He will do what He knows will bring about the best result. *If two of you agree.*

Imagine never ending another day without going together before the Father as husband and wife in prayer. Imagine stopping each other in the middle of a disagreement, and submitting yourselves to the One who can rule in this matter, changing minds and hearts until they line up with the truth. Imagine being in the middle of your next crisis, and not feeling as though you're dialing God's 9-1-1 hotline number, but simply going to the same place, doing the same thing that you always do, whether it's a good day or a bad day, a high spot or a low spot.

Do it in prayer. And "it will be done for you."

All for One

The Power of Unity

*May they all be one, as You, Father, are in Me
and I am in You. May they also be One in Us, so
the world may believe You sent Me. (John 17:21)*

God is One.

The Bible centers around this mysterious truth that God—triune as Father, Son, and Spirit—is still One in ultimate reality.

We see a glimpse of this in the first chapter of Genesis, where God said, "Let Us make man in Our image, according to Our likeness" (v. 26). We see it in Matthew 3, where Jesus emerged from the waters of baptism to the thunderous acclaim of His Father's voice, booming from heaven, "This is My beloved Son," even as the Spirit of God, "descending like a dove," came down on Him in power (vv. 16–17).

We can't quite understand it. Even with this marvelous brain equipment we've been given, able to think both concretely and abstractly, the Trinity is one of those biblical doctrines we can only follow so far before our systems simply run out of connections we can make. We get the egg thing (eggshell, egg yolk, egg white—still one egg). We get the ice thing (solid, liquid, gas—all still water). But those are just pictures. The actual concept still blows our minds.

But "listen, Israel," said Moses to the people of Abraham, Isaac, and Jacob, "the LORD our God, the LORD is One" (Deut. 6:4). He exists in such perfect unity that it can rightly be said of Him that He is Three in One.

Just as it can rightly be said of you and your spouse that, although you are two distinct individuals, He has made you "one flesh" (Eph. 5:31).

You are one.

Let's think a little bit today about what that means. Paul made this truth the basis of his appeal for how we should treat one another in marriage. "Husbands are to love their wives as their own bodies. He who loves his wife loves himself. For no one ever hates his own flesh but provides and cares for it" (Eph. 5:28–29). Since you and your mate are one flesh now, anything you do that hurts or frightens or distresses him or her, you're doing it to yourself. As well.

When their heart feels heavy, yours should feel heavy too. When their body aches from a difficult health condition or a recovery from surgery, so does yours, sort of. If you happen to speak harshly to them, or speak derogatorily about them to others, or even think unkind thoughts about them in the privacy of your own mind, doing those little fake arguments in your head or against the inside windshield of the car, consider how it would feel if they were to do that to *you*—because that's precisely what's happening. You're being ugly to *yourself.* You're being dismissive of *yourself.* You're poking and prodding and causing pain to *yourself.* And nobody does that—not in their right mind. That's why we shouldn't do it to one another.

Of course, the opposite is equally true—and provides an extra layer of motivation for dealing tenderly and patiently and lovingly with your mate. Again, it's because caring for them is like caring for yourself. Forgiving them is like forgiving yourself. Listening to them, supporting their passions, rubbing their shoulders, telling them you like their new haircut. Isn't that what you want for yourself? Truth is, it's much more likely you'll *get* that for yourself if you start being the one who loves them as yourself.

Paul also mentioned another area along these lines—not always popular, though sometimes *wildly* popular—concerning our obligations toward satisfying the sexual needs of our mate. "A husband should fulfill his marital responsibility to his wife, and likewise a wife to her husband. A wife does not have the right over her own body, but her husband does. In the same way, a husband does not have the right over his own body, but his wife does" (1 Cor. 7:3–4). The upshot of all this: "Do not deprive one another sexually—except when you agree for a time, to devote yourselves to prayer. Then come together again; otherwise, Satan may tempt you because of your lack of self-control" (v. 5).

So there you have it. Did you know the Bible talked like that? Read the Song of Solomon sometime, and realize it's not just some kind of spiritualized analogy about Christ's love for

His church. It is indeed a celebration of married love, all the way into the bedroom. After all, why *shouldn't* the Scripture show us and teach us how these sexual natures and desires of ours are meant to be done *right*, rather than only warning against immorality and telling us what not to do.

Being one flesh makes a difference.

Being united changes how we treat each other.

We talked a few chapters ago about the primary message of marriage—how it presents to others a living portrait of Christ's unconditional, covenant love for His church, His bride. Jesus said in John 17 that unity among believers communicates a message as well. "May they also be one in Us," He prayed to the Father, "so the world may believe You sent Me" (v. 21). "May they be made completely one, so the world may know You have sent Me and have loved them as You have loved Me" (v. 23).

Being united as "one flesh" in marriage can do that too. When we love one another with the same care and forethought and consideration and understanding as we would treat ourselves in the same situation, the unity shows. The love of Christ beams through us.

And both we and our mates experience being loved.

Like they're the one and only. Because they are.

Day 16

Glad We Got That Settled

Resolving Conflict

We must pursue what promotes peace and what builds up one another. (Romans 14:19)

Every marriage comes with the raw material for conflict and discord. Some couples, of course, end up struggling with it more than others. But the difference is only in degree. No home is a conflict-free zone. And whatever form the particulars take at your house—those repeated tremors that can easily, repeatedly roil the waters of anger and opposition for you and your spouse—they are as serious for you as others' issues are for them. The thing that one person might consider easy to handle is what can nearly undo somebody else.

In his book *The Negotiator*, former U.S. Senator George Mitchell recounts his years of experience as a leading diplomat, seeking compromise and agreement among all kinds of battling factions. Once, after accepting a presidential request to serve as a special envoy to the Middle East, he was speaking at an event in Jerusalem. During his talk, he mentioned how he had recently helped broker a peace agreement among the feuding parties in Northern Ireland, a violent clash of wills and agendas that had gone on for eight hundred years. He hoped his success in that part of the world would serve as inspiration for making strides in the long, embittered history of Jewish-Arab relations.

When he finished speaking, a local Israeli man approached him. "Did you say eight hundred years?" he asked. *Mm-hmm, that's right.* "Eight hundred years . . ." the man repeated. "Such a recent argument. No wonder you settled it."

Your triggers as a couple may be the marriage equivalent of the eight-hundred-year kind. Or the four-thousand-year kind. Or maybe just the ten-days to two-weeks kind. But settling them, learning to navigate them, can be as much of a challenge for you as for another.

Thankfully the Bible is a full-length story of conflict, which shows us we're not alone in some of the responses we often take. Adam and Eve, for instance, chose the now time-honored reflex of dodging and hiding and trying to pretend nothing was wrong. Maybe if they didn't think about it, or admit to their part in it, the whole thing would just go away. (Doesn't work so well.) When the Lord refused to ignore the root of the problem, however, they went immediately into blaming mode—Adam even blaming God for "the woman You gave to be with me" (Gen. 3:12).

That doesn't work so well either.

But while seeing ourselves in many of these biblical events, we also see better methods for resolving our quarrels. Abraham, for example, in trying to defuse a spat between himself and his nephew Lot over grazing land, simply took the high road, letting Lot have first pick of the territory. "If you go to the left, I will go to the right; if you go to the right, I will go to the left" (Gen. 13:9). Some battles, Abraham realized, just aren't worth winning.

Esau, in another event, noting his brother Jacob's hemming/hawing way of trying to feel him out after years of unresolved anger, cut through the circular sense of avoidance. He ran to meet him, "hugged him, threw his arms around him"—the whole bit (Gen. 33:4). Life was too short to keep this thing simmering. Let's just put it to rest and get on to getting along.

Obviously not everything can (nor should) be swept under the rug or given in to, even though that's sometimes the best way to get past it. The instruction we receive from Scripture is to "walk in the light" (1 John 1:7). "Everything exposed by the light is made clear, for what makes everything clear is light" (Eph. 5:13–14). Stuffing things into shadow and darkness is not how serious matters are solved. The light provides the setting where healthy discussion can happen, where healing can occur, where the truth can be accurately judged, and where others can get involved in helping us, if necessary.

But even though we will always come across issues that prove resistant to resolution, our attitude is what will often spell the difference in how things go and progress.

Stay calm. The worst things are usually said second or third after the first unfiltered comment. And none of them would probably have entered into it at all if this conversation had remained a coolheaded attempt at understanding. "A hot-tempered man stirs up conflict, but a man slow to anger calms strife" (Prov. 15:18).

Say only what's helpful. We can't control what our wife or husband may do or say, but we can keep our own words few and keep ourselves in check, "not paying back evil for evil or insult for insult but, on the contrary, giving a blessing" (1 Pet. 3:9).

Strive for peace. The goal from the outset of any kind of confrontation or misunderstanding should be to reclaim harmony from where it's been lost to discord. "If possible on your part, live at peace with everyone" (Rom. 12:18).

Seek an end. The longer these things are allowed to stew and gather momentum, the harder they become to untangle. Too much other stuff gets embedded inside. Fearlessly work toward a conclusion, rather than continuing to debate the same old set of points, over and over again. "Don't let the sun go down on your anger, and don't give the Devil an opportunity" (Eph. 4:26–27).

Marriage requires a lot of energy, battling against a steady stream of outside opposition that seeks to eat away at your unity. Why waste it fighting each other, when you can pursue loving agreement with each other at much less cost? And with much less fuss.

Day 17

People of God
You and the Church

Let us be concerned about one another in order to promote love and good works, not staying away from our worship meetings, as some habitually do. (Hebrews 10:24–25)

Here's hoping you're actively participating already in a solid church not too far from where you live, one that faithfully teaches the Word and provides you opportunity for growing in Christ, utilizing your spiritual gifts in service to the body. No church is perfect, of course. (It's got people in it—hey, it's got *us* in it.) But we honor and obey the Lord by joining together with each other in worship, in fellowship, in learning, and in ministry.

In too many cases, however, church is just a place to go—to hear the message, to feel the singing, to give the kids a class to attend where they'll hear the Bible and hopefully learn something valuable. Church, though—as you know—is meant to be much more than just a weekly or every-so-often event for you as a couple. The church is your *community of faith*.

Of course it's bigger than one street address, big enough to include Christians from other congregations as well. The larger Church—the capital letter-*C* Church—is a vibrant and powerful thing. As part of *this* Church, we're united with believers in South Africa and the Philippines and Philadelphia and Fort Lauderdale and everywhere that Jesus lives in the hearts of men. And yet this single collection of people who call your particular church their home provides you and your marriage a place to be grounded, to be accountable, to personally give and receive the kind of friendship that helps you live out the gospel in an ongoing, responsible fashion.

It's a place where people count on you, and where you count on them too. A place where you don't fall off their radars, and you don't let them fall off yours.

Your church is a commitment. It's a promise.

A promise *from* you and a promise *to* you.

The church is a lifestyle of loving and sharing together. Of uniting in kingdom work and priorities together. Of studying God's Word together. Of praying and listening and laughing—of doing your lives together.

Of developing relationships that cross generations. Of challenging each other from the Scriptures in how to think and act and respond and raise your children. We celebrate each other's weddings. Dedicate each other's babies. Bury each other's dead. And hug each other's necks at times when we need each other's presence more than we actually need each other's words.

Look back at how the New Testament church was lived out in its earliest days of existence (Acts 2:41–47). Granted, it wasn't perfect either. They quickly ran into a number of problems that revealed their weaknesses and required new adjustments. So we shouldn't hold them up as a lost ideal, as if modeling their identical pattern is our main goal. And yet theirs was obviously an exciting group to hang around and be part of. Christ was central not only to their lives as individuals but to their union as His followers.

The spiritually lost were consistently being drawn to saving faith through their witness—every day, all the time. They met each other's needs, confident that they, too, could depend on help from their Christian family if they found themselves in a pinch. They were singularly focused on what God was doing in their midst, devoting their time and energies to eternally minded pursuits. Words of praise and prayer were on their lips everywhere they went.

These were the people they most enjoyed spending time with—because these people shared a bond that went beyond friendship, beyond common interests. These people were family in ways that not even family can be.

Brothers. Sisters. Fathers. Mothers.

Living it out. Being the church.

Your marriage needs that.

One of the truly significant shifts of church history occurred—we're talking hundreds and hundreds of years ago—when believers began to view themselves as being less and less dependent on the religious leadership for their entire sense of relationship with God. The availability of the printed Bible, the movement from clergy-based systems to more congregational governance, toward theological reformation— all these things and more contributed to it. Over the course of time, Christians rightly began taking more ownership of their spiritual lives and growth. Toss a little 1960s and '70s into the mix, and you come out with "quiet time" as being a foundational expectation of normal, daily, accepted Christian living.

And that's great. Be sure you're doing that. More and more of that.

But our Enemy will look for any opening he can find, even if it's a good and noble one, to try stealing things away from us. And one of the more subtle, seductive ways he's worked against us is by tricking us into elevating our one-on-one fellowship with God until (if we're not careful) it can replace our sense of need for the church, for being together in worship, for serving alongside each other, for growing within an overall body, not just as an isolated body part.

So the words of Hebrews are as relevant today as when written centuries ago: "Let us be concerned about one another in order to promote love and good works, not staying away from our worship meetings, as some habitually do, but encouraging each other, and all the more as you see the day drawing near" (10:24–25).

Christian marriage is not just for the two of you. It's for the two of you to be joined with the rest of us in being the family of God.

Day 18

Buried Treasure
Choosing Gratitude

*Let the peace of the Messiah, to which you
were also called in one body, control your
hearts. Be thankful. (Colossians 3:15)*

Those three little words? "I love you"? The ones that
every wife and husband love to hear? Your spouse
would probably do an even swap with you today for
only *two* words, as long as they were some variation of "Thank
you."

Or even just one word.

"Thanks."

"Thanks for filling up the windshield wiper stuff in my
car. I meant to tell you it had run out." *You're welcome.* "Thank
you for putting the clean silverware away. I hate doing that
part when I unload the dishwasher, for some reason. Isn't that

weird?" *Ha, I know. I don't mind.* "Thank you for listening. I really needed that. It helped so much to talk to you." *Wish I could do more.* "Thanks for being so patient with how long this is taking to clear up." *I know you're doing the best you can, hon.*

"Thank you."

Mmm . . . love hearing that.

It means you noticed. It means you weren't just sitting there focused on the one or two things you could find to be critical about—which usually aren't that hard to find. You chose instead to isolate some of the qualities in your man or your woman that you appreciate. "Thank you."

It means you care. It means you're committed to the growth of this relationship, that you're looking for ways to keep your marriage fresh and revitalized. You're willing to accept the reality that your spouse (like you) is a flawed human being. And you realize the best way to help them grow, to aspire, to become more of the person you want them to be is by investing your love in them, not goading them with your constant criticism. "Thank you."

But more than anything, it means you're obeying the Lord, obeying His Word . . . because His command to you—His command to all of us—is to "be thankful."

Part of the sacrificial system instituted in the Old Testament law included "thank offerings" (2 Chron. 33:16), voluntary expressions of gratitude toward God. The psalms regularly encourage us to show our thankfulness to Him, to "sacrifice a thank offering to God" (Ps. 50:14). "Whoever sacrifices a thank offering honors Me," He said (Ps. 50:23). Jeremiah, in one of his prophecies concerning Israel's restoration from exile and from the hard consequences of its sin, linked the bringing of "thank offerings to the temple" as part of how God would "restore the fortunes of the land as in former times" (Jer. 33:11).

And maybe we can find a clue here ourselves for how to increase our gratitude toward each other, as well . . . because being openly thankful toward our mate is at its heart an expression of gratitude toward God.

You remember from grammar class, when discussing the four different types of sentences—(1) normal declarative sentences, (2) questions, (3) commands, and (4) exclamations— the subject of a *command* or an *imperative* sentence is an understood "you." In other words, if you were to hand this book to your spouse and say, "Here, read this part about how you're supposed to be more thankful for me," the subject of that sentence is a word that doesn't even appear. "(*You*) read this part . . ." (except don't really say that).

Similarly, every time you thank your wife or your husband for taking out the trash, or preparing such a delicious meal, or being such a great parent, or not getting upset with you for accidentally sitting on their sunglasses, you're actually thanking *God* for them and for all of that, without actually mentioning His name.

In fact, that's what makes Christian gratitude so much more special than the glass-half-full, go-around-the-table expressions of thanksgiving that just anybody can give. The *real* joy of gratitude is being able to deliver it directly to the appropriate address—not to your lucky stars or to the good hand you've been dealt, but to God Himself as the giver of "every generous act and every perfect gift" (James 1:17). To be thankful for your spouse, to affirm and appreciate them for even the most minor of things, is in truth another opportunity for you to worship and praise your gracious God for putting this one special person in your life.

Life is a battle. All of us, every day, are waging spiritual war against our own sins and temptations. We're also fighting the encroaching demands of workloads, outside responsibilities, and lifestyle expectations, as well as various combinations of regrets, insecurities, hurtful memories, and other sinister intrusions. And while we don't want our spouse to make a project of us, where we can tell they're artificially looking for ways to make us feel better, we do need home to be a place where our attempts at thoughtfulness and protectiveness and other loving marks of maturity don't completely go unmentioned, or are even replaced by being picked at for something else.

"As you have received Christ Jesus the Lord, walk in Him, rooted and built up in Him and established in the faith, just as you were taught, overflowing with gratitude" (Col. 2:6–7). And make sure *some* of that gratitude—no, maybe a whole *lot* of that gratitude—flows past your mate on its way to becoming praise at the throne room of God.

Day 19

Open House

Practicing Hospitality

*Don't neglect to show hospitality, for by doing
this some have welcomed angels as guests
without knowing it. (Hebrews 13:2)*

Perhaps you're one of those people who can't think of anything you'd enjoy much more this weekend than having a bunch of people at your house for a cookout, or having your parents or one of your siblings and their families pass through town and come to stay with you. You'd feel the excitement building as you put clean sheets on the bed or folded a fresh set of towels in the bathroom. You'd love going to the grocery and picking out the things they enjoy eating and snacking on, the things you could serve special for them at breakfast on Saturday morning.

Sound like fun?

Okay, maybe not to everybody. Perhaps the prevailing moods that sweep around *your* shoulders when you think about needing to entertain company are panic, dread, the fear of being critiqued, and the overwhelming responsibility for keeping everybody satisfied and comfortable.

And you know what? This is really not a matter of right and wrong, of superior character versus selfish resistance or people avoidance. Paul said that among the spiritual gifts the Lord bestows on His people are those of "service" and "giving" (Rom. 12:7–8)—God-inspired levels of caring for others that exceed what another person may be equipped to do, whose spiritual giftedness lies somewhere else. Plus, each of us enters adulthood having been exposed to certain growing-up experiences that make us either more or less at ease with the demands of hospitality, not to mention our own inborn temperaments. Some of us like things loud and boisterous; others much prefer the quiet, just being alone. And again, nothing wrong with that. With either of those. Or with any placement of our personality along the spectrum.

But just as people who are especially called and blessed with the gift of evangelism (Eph. 4:11) don't disqualify the rest of us from being obedient to the Great Commission (Matt. 28:19–20), those who more naturally excel at being gracious hosts are not excuses for why the rest of us can keep to ourselves and close our doors to the outside world.

Our homes are places of ministry.

That's because our marriages are not only meant to meet our own needs through each other but are also meant to be outward facing as well. God's reasons for putting us together go far beyond just making us happy to be loved by someone. He also desires for our relationship to become a means of bringing light and joy and blessing and goodness into the lives of those around us. We are witnesses of His grace. We are witnesses of His fullness. We are witnesses of His Son and of the difference He makes in our lives, as well as in our homes and in how we live out this gift we call our marriage and family.

So we should see our current address and living situation as an outpost of opportunity. Even if it's a tiny little one- or two-bedroom apartment. Even if our kitchen countertops and bathroom fixtures aren't the latest thing in contemporary design. Some of us may never feel overly confident when asking people over. We might sit up late the night before, worrying over things that others don't even think about. But we can still, without succumbing to any implied pressure to be like anybody else, make our home an open place where people are welcome to come and visit, even if primarily in small increments of one or two or three at a time. For coffee and store-bought dessert. For nice, unrushed conversation. For God and for His glory.

If marriage was intended to exist on its own little island, where all we were supposed to do was to feed into each other, God could certainly have created it that way. Instead, He chose to drop us into a world of existing relationships and an ever-expanding grid of new friendships and connections.

And while we must be sure to stay aware of not losing ourselves to what other people want or expect of us, our marriages actually grow deeper and richer by absorbing the experiences of outside interaction. It brings new questions into our lives to be pondered and answered. It broadens our scope of thinking. It draws out of us an ability to speak into the lives of others—a one-on-one brand of sharing and wisdom we didn't even know we possessed or could give. But by making ourselves and our marriage available to Him, constantly being offered up to Him, where *He* decides—not us—the kinds of opportunities He wants to create around our kitchen tables and sofas and patio furniture, our relationship as husband and wife becomes an even stronger bond.

"Share with the saints in their needs," Paul said, and "pursue hospitality" (Rom. 12:13). Create those kinds of moments for entertaining "angels unawares" (Heb. 13:2 KJV), where the timing and the setting and the steam coming off your teapot can put people in just the right frame of mind for opening up to you, seeking God with you, and bringing a different kind of flavor into your home for the evening or afternoon.

This doesn't need to cost you two hundred dollars in food and cups and cake and decorations. It doesn't need to be every week or all the time. But your marriage will benefit from being seen on the inside. And you will be a blessing to the Lord and to others by letting Him have what's already in your hand to give, and to open it up for the miracles He can work inside of it.

Day 20

With My Complements

Roles in Marriage

To sum up, each one of you is to love his wife as himself, and the wife is to respect her husband. (Ephesians 5:33)

et's start by making an obvious statement. God is not the least bit worried about how His message is perceived. He doesn't employ a poll tracking service. He doesn't need a spin doctor. He's not concerned how statements first made for human consumption in the first century AD will play amid the hypersensitive, hypercritical context of the twenty-first century.

God is God; the truth is the truth; and that's really all that matters.

So while we could take up today's space trying to edit His Word to suit the tastes of our modern ears, something should probably tell us (like the Holy Spirit, for example) that we're always much better off when we just let the Scripture speak for itself.

Men. Women. We're different.

Are we still allowed to say that?

Once it was obvious just by looking at us. We simply understood. But with today's blurring of sexual identities, and with a push toward equality that not even the most ardent activists of an earlier age could likely have foreseen, the face of change has become the new normal. In the workplace, in the military, in sports, even in the public restroom—men and women are now increasingly expected to occupy the same places.

And that would be fine, I guess.

If men and women weren't different.

Yet we are. Different. Not superior. Not inferior. Paul said as Christians, "there is no Jew or Greek, slave or free, male or female; for you are all one in Christ Jesus" (Gal. 3:28). We're not of higher or lower value in the eyes of God, nor in the eyes of each other and of society. But we *are* different.

Like both sides of a pair of scissors are different. Like both ends of a garden hose are different. Like the male and female ends of an electrical cord or an AV connector are different. They wouldn't work if they weren't different, if both were exactly the same. We *need* their differences, or else we couldn't cut our coupons, water the flowers, plug in the toaster, or watch the television.

Our differences *complement* one another.

That's simply how God has made us.

And how He's made marriage too.

So when God's Word says, "Wives, submit to your own husbands as to the Lord . . . as the church submits to Christ" (Eph. 5:22, 24), He is not demeaning women but is actually ascribing great value to her as the female partner in a marriage. He is giving her an incredibly difficult, important challenge and responsibility.

He gives husbands one as well. "Husbands, love your wives, just as Christ loved the church and gave Himself for her" (v. 25). This doesn't make men better or of more significance than their wives, but it identifies the different kind of role that husbands are commanded to embody in their homes.

And if this worked as outlined—husbands loving their wives with complete unselfishness; wives submitting to their husbands with complete trust—everyone would be in a place of maximum blessing and safety. Wives wouldn't be overruled by overbearing men who don't care about anybody but themselves. Husbands would be so sensitive to God's leadership, so self-sacrificial in their desire to love their wives, that no one would feel the need to resist.

And though our sinful human natures prevent this ideal from ever becoming exactly what it could be, the beauty of what God can do through us when we dedicate ourselves to drawing closer and closer to it is where our greatest fulfillment in marriage lies.

So . . . submission. Within this biblical frame, it doesn't mean women are to keep their mouths shut and never make a peep, just go along with what their husband says. Nor does it mean that men, simply by virtue of being male, automatically know what to do in any situation and are therefore tasked with being the unilateral, undisputed leaders of their homes . . . always the smartest person in the room. How could a husband *love* his wife well without *knowing* her well, without possessing an appreciation for her discernment and opinions, without wanting to be sure anything he did was a net gain for her?

Yet even in a marriage where the husband is not particularly loving or faithful, the Word does instruct wives to "submit yourselves to your own husbands so that, even if some disobey the Christian message, they may be won over without a message by the way their wives live when they observe your pure, reverent lives" (1 Pet. 3:1–2). Yes, you may give up some privileges and preferences in cases like these. And, yes, certain situations do exist in which submission is too physically or emotionally dangerous to keep attempting without someone on the outside having knowledge of what's going on. But the way to change a man is rarely through confrontation and disrespectful refusal; it's through love and patience and prayerful, persevering sacrifice—just as husbands must continue to show their wives "honor as coheirs of the grace of life" (1 Pet. 3:7), even when the relationship is rocky.

We're different. But we're supposed to be. And that's okay . . . because our differences are what make us come together so beautifully.

Day 21

Lifelong Learning
Acquiring Mentors

Listen to counsel and receive instruction so that you may be wise in later life. (Proverbs 19:20)

Assuming you're not already eighty-five years old—in which case *you* should be the one writing this book so we can read what *you* have to say—you likely have easy, personal access to people who are a generation or more ahead of you. Whether at church or in your neighborhood, maybe a grandparent or an older relative, you wouldn't have any trouble locating someone twenty, thirty, or forty years older than you, who would gladly accept your invitation for coffee, lunch, or dinner, just to talk.

Only you wouldn't be doing it "just to talk." And maybe you wouldn't be doing it just this once. What if you had someone who met with you every few months, or maybe twice a year—someone you respect for their spiritual example, someone whose marriage inspires you—so that you could lob questions at them and learn from what they might volley back?

And what if you and your spouse had a couple who served this same kind of function for both of you together—a treasured husband and wife whose top-of-mind answers to one evening's worth of questions could be more valuable to you than a whole year's worth of Wednesday-night small-group classes?

The obvious thing is how much sense these kinds of relationships make. The most staggering thing is how few of them actually occur.

Why is that? Is it because nobody has time for you? Because nobody's interested? Because they hate sharing their stories and being asked their opinions? No way. *Big* no way. The truth is, even though a majority of people who fit into this older/mentor category would probably question whether anything they said to you would be of much use, they would actually be thrilled—honored—if you were to ask them.

Now, they're not likely to ask *you*. They're not going to be the one to approach and say they've seen some things in your life that they could help you with. But if *you* made the first move, you and they could probably get started talking by next weekend or sooner.

Wouldn't that be great?

A real gift to your marriage?

The Bible endorses and champions these kinds of age-limitless relationships. Paul, in writing to a pastor he'd installed on the island of Crete, mentioned the kinds of qualities that are supposed to be present in mature believers.

"Older men are to be level headed, worthy of respect, sensible, and sound in faith, love, and endurance. In the same way, older women are to be reverent in behavior, not slanderers, not addicted to much wine" (Titus 2:2–3). I'll bet you could think of some people right this second who embody every single one of these character traits. They've lived in such a way, faithfully over the long haul, that their bucket of admirable qualities is filled to the brim.

But here's what they've been commanded to do with all of that. "They are to teach what is good, so they may encourage the young women to love their husbands and to love their children, to be self-controlled, pure, homemakers, kind, and submissive to their husbands, so that God's message will not be slandered" (vv. 3–5). The older men? Same thing. They are to "encourage the young men to be self-controlled in everything. Make yourself an example of good works with integrity and dignity in your teaching" (v. 6–7). This download of lessons learned is meant to be an expected, ongoing, life-on-life appointment within the church family, across the generations.

But they need somebody to share it with.

And why shouldn't that somebody be you?

So when will you start, if you haven't already? Who will you ask? And what would you like to ask them?

You could ask their advice on a current struggle you're undergoing. *Did you ever deal with anything like this? How did you handle it?* You could share the details of a decision you're needing to make. *What do you think we should expect, whichever way we end up going? What are we perhaps not seeing, not thinking long-term enough?* You could talk about the life stages your kids are in, and how you're trying to parent them through it. *Remember when your children were this age? What would you do different if you could go back and do it again?*

Perhaps that's one of the things they wish the most—that they could go back and do it again. Do it better. Do it with more wisdom, appreciation, and patience. And you are one way they can sort of *do* that. By giving you the benefit of their hard lessons. By helping you avoid some of the same traps they fell into. By pointing you to Scriptures that speak to these very issues, places you may not have noticed . . . but if you *did* notice and could hear God speaking to you through them, you and your spouse could walk right into blessing instead of peeling off into danger.

"The glory of young men is their strength," says one of the proverbs—your energetic ability to engage with life's challenges, your opportunities to affect so many potential outcomes. But "the splendor of old men is gray hair" (Prov. 20:29)—their years of learning and observing, of growing in wisdom, of seeing firsthand what God can do.

Put this kind of "glory" and "splendor" in the same room, at the same time, and you and your marriage won't be able to help but grow stronger and stronger from the interchange.

Day 22

Did You Hear That?

Learning to Listen

Lord, listen to my voice; let Your ears be
attentive to my cry for help. (Psalm 130:2)

We really must want to be heard.

And God really must want to hear us.

Otherwise there's no explanation for why His Word is so full of instances where people called out to Him in prayer, needing help, needing to talk, needing to be convinced their problems and questions were not simply being ignored, out of hand, undelivered, straight into file thirteen. Yet again and again, the Bible confirms that our God in heaven hears.

He listens. To us.

"This poor man cried, and the LORD heard him and saved him from all his troubles" (Ps. 34:6). "I called to the LORD in my distress, and I cried to my God for help. From His temple He heard my voice, and my cry to Him reached His ears" (Ps. 18:6). "May the LORD be praised, for He has heard the sound of my pleading" (Ps. 28:6). "LORD, you have heard the desire of the humble; You will strengthen their hearts. You will listen carefully" (Ps. 10:17).

God is an unabashed, unapologetic listener. Imagine that. Even with all the people who right this minute are bombarding His throne with their cries, their fears, their worries, their desperation, He still is listening. To all of us. In fact, from His unique position outside of time, where no limits exist that would keep Him from being able to hear everything we're saying, all at once, He literally has all the time in the world for us. To listen to us. To respond to us. To wait while we try to get the words out, the best we can.

So . . .

Contemplate the implications.

If God—yes, God—has chosen to listen to us—yes, to us—what kind of arrogant right are we claiming when we are too busy, too distracted, too preoccupied, or perhaps just too disinterested to listen to what our wife or husband is saying?

Marriage is in many ways a listening art. Much of what keeps us disgruntled or disappointed with one another is driven by moments when we haven't been listening, when we've been filling in the gaps with our own conclusions and interpretations rather than truly wanting to understand what's behind our spouse's actions or responses. Yes, good listening takes time. It takes effort. It takes quieting the assumptions that form so naturally in our own head. It takes shutting down the loud, demanding, invasive parasites of outside influences, those things that want to take up all our oxygen and brain cells, maxing out our attention span.

But listening is actually a time-saving enterprise. A single hour, invested entirely into listening to whatever's on the mind and heart of our spouse, may just clear up an impasse tonight that, under normal conditions, could easily linger throughout two months or more of turmoil and misunderstanding. By stopping to listen now, you could spare yourself a lot of wasted moments, detoured onto side alleys of off-the-subject conflict and conversation. Perhaps what feels the most sacrificial now is truly the best way to keep this whole thing from becoming impossibly complicated later.

The Scripture says that not listening is what gets us into most of our trouble in life. Moses said to the children of Israel, "If your heart turns away and you do not listen and you are led astray to bow down to other gods and worship them, I tell you today that you will certainly perish and will not live long in the land you are entering to possess" (Deut. 30:17–18). The Lord said He had commanded them to "obey Me, and then I will be your God, and you will be My people. You must follow every way I command you so that it may go well with you. Yet they didn't listen or pay attention." Instead, they "followed their own advice," choosing to live in accordance with "their own stubborn, evil heart. They went backward and not forward" (Jer. 7:23–24).

Backward. Not forward.

And that's exactly what *we* can expect as well, in our own homes and marriages, if we quit listening to one another, if we think we've already heard enough, if we believe we can play our part just fine without needing to sit down and hear . . . to *really* hear . . . what the other is actually saying. Not listening is always a bad step in the wrong direction.

"My people did not listen to Me," God said in another place, "Israel did not obey Me. So I gave them over to their stubborn hearts to follow their own plans" (Ps. 81:11–12). They found themselves not just stuck in neutral but jammed into reverse, losing the ground they'd already attained. *But,* He added, "if only My people would listen to Me and Israel would follow My ways, I would quickly subdue their enemies and turn My hand against their foes" (vv. 13–14). He would enable them to progress toward new vistas of opportunity and blessing, knocking down the many hindrances that threatened to defeat and deter them.

Listening keeps us moving ahead. And staying ahead. Listening draws us closer. It builds trust. It gives us hope that we can stay on the right track . . . or get *back* on the right track if we've been slowly wandering away, both from God and from each other.

We don't really know what's going on until we're really listening.

Day 23

Better Together

Staying Best Friends

Two are better than one because they have a good reward for their efforts. (Ecclesiastes 4:9)

Few things are much more fun than getting together with your friends.

Maybe you routinely go to lunch with a couple of people from work. Some of your favorite conversations of the week happen around and between those casual hours you spend together.

Maybe you play a sweat-dripping hour of pick-up basketball or take in an exercise class with pretty much the same group of regulars every time you go to the gym. You've gotten to know each other fairly well, and you look forward to those Tuesday and Thursday mornings—to the inside-joke relationships you've built, something you've come to really enjoy with them.

Maybe you and a tight little bunch of your closest high school or college friends still schedule a special weekend every year, getting away for some highly anticipated girl or guy time, for big laughs and old memories. You don't know how you'd keep your sanity sometimes if you didn't know this trip was coming up every spring.

And good for you. Sounds like fun. Hope you'll always be able to preserve these kinds of moments, with these kinds of friendships.

But what have you and your *spouse* been doing together lately? The same way you and these *other* folks have been doing stuff together lately?

Not because you're husband and wife, but just because you're friends?

Being "one flesh" is the spiritual reality that God created between the two of you when you pledged yourself to one another in marriage. But being friends—and becoming even *better* friends—is purely the reward of spending time together, same as with any friend. Not just living at the same address. Not just being physically present at dinnertime or at bedtime. Not just the omnipresent awareness of needing to accommodate each other's requests, as well as account for your own responsibilities. But *being* together. Working together. Serving together. Discovering new interests together. Friendship develops from including each other in more and more aspects of your life, even those you've primarily done separately or in isolation.

What might some of those areas be?

Here, we can imagine a few. What are some of the hobbies that draw you away from home one weekend or more a month?

What are some of the Bible studies and other faith-building experiences you do, which you tend to share with only a handful of other people outside your home and rarely with your own spouse? What are some of the interests your wife or husband pursues, while you're busy pursuing something else? What are some of the child-rearing obligations you delegate to one another, but that maybe you could do jointly instead . . . not only as a help to each other, but also as a way of spending more time together, devoted to the same things?

A subtle danger lurks around the edges of your relationship whenever your growth and development as an individual is primarily happening outside of what you're sharing together as a couple—for example, when you're growing spiritually with your men's or women's group, but not so much with your husband or wife. When you're becoming deeply involved in a ministry area, but perhaps at the expense of staying open and available to something else, where both of you could serve as a team. When you've got *your* friends, and your mate has *their* friends, but not many of *your* friends and *their* friends ever become what you'd call *our* friends, people both of you like to hang out with.

Life for a devoted Christian is a serious pursuit of God's will, aligning ourselves with the truth of His Word and yielding even our daily decisions to His lordship and leadership. And while we can all stay plenty busy doing a lot of good things with a lot of good people, we put ourselves in the best position for ascertaining God's will by first looking to see if it's something that builds into our marriage, something that develops this partnership He's already given us. For if chasing other goals and activities means regularly diminishing our togetherness as a couple—and if it continually meets with opposition or disapproval from what our mate wants or expects from us—we may succeed at making a lot of nice friends, but we'll run the risk of losing the one friendship in life that matters most.

Solomon wisely observed, "A man with many friends may be harmed, but there is a friend who stays closer than a brother" (Prov. 18:24). And God has given you that kind of friend—the kind that not even the closeness of blood kinship can describe or contain—by giving you a best friend in your husband or wife. Your best life will come from sowing into that friendship, allowing Him to accomplish what He desires with you while also accomplishing what He desires for your marriage.

Staying involved with other people will always be a valuable part of your life, of course—even an obedient use of your talents, dreams, and interests. Your marriage sometimes *needs* the time you spend in giving one another a chance to breathe, to encourage those things in your mate that allow them to excel and enjoy themselves, outside of your active participation with them. But don't let anything eat away at your heart of togetherness, at the common ground where you prize and prioritize the uniqueness of this relationship.

"This is my love, and this is my friend" (Song 5:16). And no one else in the world has been made to be both of those things for you.

Day 24

Gently down the Stream

Acts of Kindness

Who is wise and has understanding among you? He should show his works by good conduct with wisdom's gentleness. (James 3:13)

H ey, it's mean out there.

Mean.

You're stuck in the passing lane, for example, with no way to get over at the moment, not with this rush-hour press of traffic. Still, you're inching up to ten miles over the speed limit, just to try to find an opening you can squeeze your car into. But the look of that guy's face in your rearview mirror, flashing his high beams off and on, creeping up on your bumper, motioning where he wants you to go—as if that's not the *only* thing he's motioning for you to do . . .

Boy, you've really made him mad.

Mean.

You've felt the same sort of presence in line at the cash register, checking their watch, shifting their weight, huffing their displeasure at the amount of time this transaction ahead of them is taking. You've watched them talking on top of each other on the cable TV news shows, while the moderator tries to quiet the loudest voice from continuing to rant so that both of them can have a chance to be heard. Perhaps you've endured the full weight of their frustration in the workplace, coming down from someone who's in a position of authority over you, where nothing you do seems to ever quite enough to satisfy them, where there's always something they're hot about or expecting more of.

It can get pretty rough.

Mean.

Which *means* the last thing you really need when you get home from being out there all day is somebody else who's liable to be, you know . . .

Mean.

Now nobody's claiming that your mate can't sometimes be a bit annoying. Some of their habits, some of their abruptness, some of their ways of being thoughtless and forgetful—even if they do it by accident—it can be hard to swallow and accept with a smile. But how often has a biting word from you delivered the kind of apology or admittance of fault that you think you deserve? How many times has your irritation only amplified the problem into an issue that took you the rest of the night to get over? Maybe you're *still* not quite over it.

But maybe there's a gentler way . . .

The apostle Peter, writing specifically to wives, but addressing a character trait that is certainly admirable in husbands as well, talked about the "imperishable quality of a gentle and quiet spirit, which is very valuable in God's eyes" (1 Pet. 3:4). We know he was talking about something that's meant to be present in each of us, because he soon counseled these same believers not to get angry at people who insulted them for their allegiance with Christ. They should answer them instead, he told them, with "gentleness and respect, keeping your conscience clear" (v. 16). Showing gentle restraint is representative of the One we serve.

Jesus, for example, said to "come to Me, all of you who are weary and burdened, and I will give you rest . . . because I am gentle and humble in heart, and you will find rest for yourselves" (Matt. 11:28–29). The only reason any of us are standing here today with forgiven hearts and eternal hopes is because of the "kindness" the Father has extended to us in Christ Jesus (Eph. 2:7)—a "kindness" He continues to show us in order to keep leading us to repentance (Rom. 2:4).

We can read other places in Scripture, of course, where His approach toward us is more corrective and confrontational. That's because He alone, from His position of perfect knowledge, knows exactly what's required for getting through to us at a given moment in time, seeking to wake us up from our stupor, to alter the foolish course we're traveling. But you and I—we're hardly in the same position over our mates as God occupies. As heavenly Father, He is well within His rights to enforce His Word upon them (upon *each* of us), even if the cost of these consequences can sometimes be quite heavy to bear.

But rarely does your spouse need as much toughness and sternness from you as they need your gentleness, your kindness, the soft cushion of your love. Rarely is their intention to deliberately cause harm to you but is more likely the result of pressure from another source, of frustration from another event. And while your gentleness may not produce the immediate effect you wanted to see, or may not keep the result of their action from stinging your heart a bit right now, the outcome created over time through your gentleness is almost sure to end up capturing their attention and motivating them to change. "A gentle tongue can break a bone," the proverb says (Prov. 25:15). Those who wish to "restore" someone to their spiritual senses are told to approach them with a "gentle spirit" (Gal. 6:1).

When your wife or husband sees you next, they're likely to be fresh from some kind of experience where they've been hassled by someone's demands, disappointed by their own failings, fatigued by their daily obligations, or beset by difficulties at least somewhat beyond their control. And if you were in their shoes, looking into your face, what do you think you'd most want to see and hear?

A gentle look. A gentle word.

Say it like you mean it.

Day 25

Worth Celebrating

Building Traditions

*Speak to the Israelites and tell them: These are My
appointed times, the times of the LORD that you
will proclaim as sacred assemblies. (Leviticus 23:2)*

Maybe you and your spouse are more the spontaneous type. You don't go in for a lot of form, custom, and ceremony. The more casual and low-key, the better. And that's fine. Not everyone's born to be a party planner. And those who *are*—they can often get so wrapped up in the details of what they're producing that they lose the greater purpose behind it. Just because something looks all fancy doesn't make it any more special than barbecue and baked beans on a paper plate.

But even a cursory reading of the Old Testament reveals how God deliberately created special moments and seasons as part of the rhythm of the annual calendar, significant events that He wanted His people to observe.

The weekly Sabbath, for example, a day for "complete rest, a sacred assembly" (Lev. 23:3). The Passover and Festival of Unleavened Bread, a seven-day commemoration of Israel's deliverance from Egypt (vv. 5–8). The Festival of Harvest, also known as Pentecost—fifty days following Passover (a week of weeks)—to celebrate the giving of the law as well as the first yield of the wheat harvest (vv. 15–21). And on and on it went—Rosh Hashanah, the new year (vv. 23–25); Yom Kippur, the Day of Atonement (vv. 26–33); the Festival of Booths or Tabernacles, a weeklong remembrance of their wilderness wanderings (vv. 33–43)—and more.

These events, of course, contained not only patriotic importance to Israel but also spiritual significance for all of God's people. They proved prophetic of the coming of Christ, the giving of the Holy Spirit, and other ramifications of the gospel that would become gloriously fulfilled in coming generations. Yet even as we continue to celebrate Communion in our churches today, obediently reminding ourselves of the price of our salvation and the living hope of our resurrection, the keeping of traditions is not a useless formality or exercise. When kept alive by the deeper meaning of what a ceremony like the Lord's Supper represents, it remains not just a ritual to do but a valuable, necessary part of keeping us grounded in what's true, in what we desire by God's help to keep pursuing.

Now, as believers in Christ, of course, our security in Him is not determined by any kind of law-keeping performance. We're not made any more holy and blameless before Him by doing certain things. Yet because we're so irritatingly forgetful, and because we've been created with internal clocks that respond to the marking of time, we can experience some tangible blessings from making much of certain happenings and events.

And maybe our marriages could benefit from some of those too.

Sure, we could sail through every day of the year without considering any one of those days as being more special than another. If we miss an anniversary here and there, if we can't seem to find the time to celebrate it this go-round, we're no less married on the other side, right? But even with some of the extra work involved in commemorating the moment—work that may, to one or the other of you, feel like an unnecessary outlay of thought and energy—these occasions are often worth more marriage capital than they may appear.

If nothing else, they're opportunities for thanksgiving and worship. Opportunities to praise God together for what He's accomplished by blessing you with one another. If you let the moment slide with hardly a greeting card or a babysitter, you may be not only downplaying your own need for celebrating this annual event, but also allowing your appreciation toward God to go under the bridge without giving Him the honor He's due.

Forging some set-aside traditions can matter. They can provide some amazing windows for you to express your love and commitment to one another in touching, powerful, tender ways. Birthdays, for instance, can become more than just a cake-and-candles happening, but also a dedicated time of prayer and blessing. Valentine's Day, Mother's Day, and

Father's Day—you can always take advantage of retail-based holidays like these to create something more special than most.

But your life together is surely marked by dates, times, and seasons that are unique to only the two of you. The first time you met, for example. The night of your engagement. Perhaps you might even pick a certain weekend, carved out for a reason of your own choosing, that you decide is going to be your own special time for—I don't know, doing long-range planning and setting prayerful goals for the coming year.

Hey, it's your marriage. *You* decide.

And even though none of this may immediately appeal to you—or perhaps you can already hear your wife or husband shutting you down if you were to propose something like it— even a baby step in the direction of becoming more intentional, more celebratory around specific events and periods of the year, might just prove a real shot in the arm to a relationship that, left to itself, will tend to become a little dull and ordinary.

It wouldn't need to stop you from being generally off the cuff, if that's the way you guys prefer to roll. But traditions are worth creating. Your marriage is worth honoring. You'll be infusing your love with every-year opportunities for looking forward to what's coming.

You two are too special not to be celebrated.

Pure and Simple

Sexual Oneness

She was given fine linen to wear, bright and pure. For the fine linen represents the righteous acts of the saints. (Revelation 19:8)

"T he marriage of the Lamb has come" (Rev. 19:7).

That's how the closing act of history is described in the final chapters of Revelation. Christ's bride, the church, is wearing the pure, bright garments He has "given" her to wear—another testimony to the unearned, undeserved salvation He has bought for His people. "They washed their robes and made them white in the blood of the Lamb" (Rev. 7:14). They are holy. They are cleansed. They are righteous.

They are pure.

Purity. Marriage is to be marked by purity.

On one hand, we assume purity to be sort of the unspoken inheritance of marriage. Marriage, we know, is what sanctifies sexual activity, providing us the one unique, God-given relationship where we can be completely ourselves, completely unashamed, completely within the covering of His blessing. Which is true. All the frustration, guilt, or emptiness we may have felt before marriage, whether from fighting to withhold our innocence or from seeking to satisfy ourselves in illegitimate ways—marriage shows us how obedience and freedom are meant to feel when we trust God's loving, protective boundaries. We realize He's not trying to hurt us; He's actually just trying to keep us safe. He's wanting to give us more joy and fulfillment than we ever get for ourselves by trying to steal it from places where it can only cause us harm.

And yet the allure of sexual impurity doesn't just vanish into nonexistence with that one kiss we share at the altar, with that official piece of paper we sign that confirms our man-and-wife relationship. The tempter knows when we'll be ripe again for his return, when he can take advantage of our natural tendency to always want more than what we've already been given.

So marriage is not a panacea for impurity. It doesn't exempt us from needing to stay watchful of our hearts, our eyes, our thoughts, our imaginations. We are still responsible for resisting whatever insecure emotion leads us to turn our heads toward the attention and affection of another. We are still in the position of trusting God to care for us, to be enough for us, even when we're in a compromising mood for finding excuses, the ones that can justify our desire for sort of wondering what else might be out there for us.

Hopefully these kinds of stray thoughts rarely, if ever, cross your mind. Perhaps the more compelling temptations you battle—and you'd admit there are plenty of them—typically originate from a whole other spiritual zip code than that one. But if any combination of your upbringing, your memories, your biology, or your psychological makeup has created a weakness Satan can easily exploit for his favorite sexual enticements, let's decide right here and now that we are not letting him get away with it. Not with us. He can keep showing up if he wants, but he's not *getting* what he wants.

Not from us. Not anymore.

What we learn from long experience of dealing with his sneak attacks is that we don't experience the victories we desire by white-knuckling our way to obedience. Certainly we need to resist him—"Resist the Devil, and he will flee from you" (James 4:7). But the opening line of that verse—"Submit to God"—is actually our first, best line of defense. The straight-ahead commitment of "taking every thought captive to obey Christ" (2 Cor. 10:5) is where our power to walk in freedom truly comes from. The confidence of living inside the protective refuge of His love, power, and grace is how He makes us day by day stronger, building the kind of muscle He can keep infusing with obedience-seeking energy.

So instead of simply telling yourself to stop, instead of simply not wanting to bear the consequences of what impurity in thought and deed are sure to keep dredging up, instead of continually requiring the Lord's faithful discipline so you can learn your lessons and come back to your senses, pour yourself into the pure possibilities that He has opened up for you by giving you this one special person to love.

"Drink water from your own cistern, water flowing from your own well. Should your springs flow in the streets, streams of water in the public squares? They should be for you alone and not for you to share with strangers" (Prov. 5:15–17). Instead of losing again and again, keeping yourself in frames of mind where sexual distraction and temptation can find you, "be lost in her love forever" (v. 19)—be lost in his love forever. "For this is God's will, your sanctification: that you abstain from sexual immorality, so that each of you knows how to control his own body in sanctification and honor" (1 Thess. 4:3–4). "Marriage must be respected by all, and the marriage bed kept undefiled" (Heb. 13:4).

Sexual temptation is never something to underestimate or play with. "Can a man embrace fire and his clothes not be burned? Can a man walk on burning coals without scorching his feet?" (Prov. 6:27–28). But from the power base of victory that God has placed within you, and from the sanctuary of marriage He's placed around you, grasp the freedom of being able to reject all other suitors so you can invest all your love into your wife or husband. No, they may not always respond to you as you wish, but at least you'll know you're not wasting your time on foolish lies that never deliver what they offer. Here is your place. Here is your love.

Here is your exhilarating experience of purity.

Day 27

Grace and Peace
The Gift of Patience

We exhort you, brothers: warn those who are
irresponsible, comfort the discouraged, help the weak,
be patient with everyone. (1 Thessalonians 5:14)

We've spent several of these days discussing what certain people might call the softer side of marriage: *encouraging* each other, *forgiving* each other, being *grateful* for each other, showing *kindness* toward each other. Maybe you'll think it's a bit of overkill now to include yet another chapter that travels down a similar road: being *patient* with each other.

But here's the thing. Marriage is a test. Marriage tells you who you really are. Marriage confronts you with challenges that would almost always feel easier to handle by immediate reflex than by measured reflection. And after the years have intervened to rub the shine off your once-upon-a-time hesitance to speak up and say something when aggravated, soon you'll say almost anything. Usually without thinking.

So even if everyone you know would think of you as a patient person, an easygoing person, someone who's able to smoothly get along and cooperate with everybody else, the real gauge is the one that measures the temperature inside your own house—inside your own marriage—where the one person you love more than anybody else in the world can also double as the one person who gets under your skin more than anybody else in the world.

How patiently do you respond to *that* person?

Maybe the answer wouldn't matter so much if impatience ever contributed toward anything positive in marriage. Maybe it would be a moot point if impatience not only didn't fail miserably at bringing about the changes we desire in our mate, but also didn't sadly succeed at bringing about some unwanted changes in *their* mate. In us.

Nobody sets out in life, for example, to become testy, harsh, and bitter. No one, when asked who they hoped to become in adulthood, ever said they wanted to grow up to be someone who harangued their wife for putting too much sugar in her coffee or sniped at their husband for leaving the toilet seat up. You probably never saw yourself saying and griping about the things you're already finding so impossible to keep from commenting on, even if it hasn't yet reached the point where you're comparing the severity of your medical procedures to theirs. But that's precisely where you're headed—that's where this pretty face of yours is going—if you're not serious about putting your impatience out to pasture.

Impatience only breeds resistance. It only hardens our positions and widens our differences. It makes contentious issues increase in size and duration that might otherwise disintegrate under the gravity of their own weight. At the very least, it attempts to take grievances into our own hands that would certainly be more successful in the hands of the Holy Spirit, who knows—better than we do—how to get His fingers down under the real problem and lift it out of our spouse's heart while we're soundly sleeping next to them with a clear conscience.

So instead of impatience, let's practice saying some other words, inspired by what Paul the apostle said in one form or another at both the beginning and the ending of every single letter he wrote: "Grace to you and peace from God our Father and the Lord Jesus Christ" (1 Cor. 1:3).

Grace. God's grace is what each of us has been given by trusting in Christ for the forgiveness of our sins. Grace means we don't deserve it. Grace means we didn't do anything to earn it. Grace simply means He's considered our many shortcomings covered by the overwhelming tide of Christ's blood, and we are therefore released to keep growing and becoming more like Him as we steadily surrender ourselves to His lordship.

Because of grace, we've been given room to fail—not without consequence, but entirely without condemnation. Because of grace, we've been given the ongoing opportunity for repentance, rather than the ongoing remembrance of what we did before, as well as the prophetic reminder of what we'll probably do again.

And because of grace, we can extend it with a full measure of patience to our mate, believing they can become more by receiving our belief in them than our berating of them.

Peace. The presence of peace can often be a fragile experience in our homes, too easily shattered by a phone call, a financial hit, an unexpected piece of bad news. We hate those moments when something crashes into our lives to disturb the normal, settled environment that we count on for being able to function.

So we should be extra sensitive to the threats that rile up from within our own impatience, able to splinter the peace in our marriage and family by almost a single word, a raised tone of voice, a poke at a particular subject matter that we know is capable of inciting a firestorm.

"The LORD gives His people strength," David said—surely even the strength to resist chirping at a perceived slight or to overreact to an offense. And as a corollary to His strength, "the LORD blesses His people with peace" (Ps. 29:11). How could you join Him in blessing your home with even more of it today?

"Pursue peace with everyone," said the writer of Hebrews, "and holiness—without it no one will see the Lord. Make sure that no one falls short of the grace of God and that no root of bitterness springs up, causing trouble and by it, defiling many" (Heb. 12:14–15).

Let's stop looking at these character traits—encouragement, kindness, gratitude, patience—as being soft approaches to marriage. The reason they require such strength to perform is because they're actually much stronger than they seem.

Tell You the Truth

Complete Honesty

He who gives an honest answer gives a
kiss on the lips. (Proverbs 24:26)

Are you keeping anything—anything?—from your wife, from your husband . . .

Anything?

The only reasons for doing so are, honestly, not good reasons. None of them.

Embarrassment. Guilt. Fear. Worry. Shame.

See? None of them.

And yet all the reasons for breaking your silence—though perhaps risky or painful to contemplate, depending on what you're holding inside—contain some of the most significant pieces of a very complex puzzle that could finally come together to make you feel like a whole, intact person again. Maybe for the first time ever.

Just wondering what that possibility would be worth to you.

When Paul graphically depicted the suit of armor that God makes available to us for fighting our everyday battles of spiritual warfare, the first item he featured was what we've shortened to call the *belt of truth*—"truth like a belt around your waist" (Eph. 6:14). It's the leading element, the foundational piece, that helps us "stand against the tactics of the Devil" (v. 11), making us able to "resist in the evil day, and having prepared everything, to take your stand" (v. 13).

Truth. The belt of truth. It holds the whole thing together. Without it—without being anchored in the truth—nothing else fits quite right around us, even when we're trying our hardest to live like the victorious warrior we've been called and saved to be. Because how can we take our stand on truth, live as people who are unapologetically shaped by the Word, be completely open to Him and available to His Spirit, if we're not even being truthful ourselves at the core?

We can't, that's how.

But we still can. By telling the truth.

Zechariah 8 is that point in his prophetic book where, like always, God's message moves from hard warnings and consequences to promises of restoration and blessing. Sometimes, when we feel the pressure of our conscience and the conviction of God's Word weighing on us, we think He's just out to get us. This is over. He's given us all these third and fourth and fourteen hundredth chances, but apparently we've finally stepped across the line. He's bringing down the hammer, and we're smithereens when He's done.

But, no, God's heart and purpose—like all good fathers—is not to abuse and abandon His children but to bring us back into close, vibrant relationship with Him again. He's not trying to kill us; He's trying to restore us to life, even if it feels for the moment as though we might not survive His correction.

So in this pivotal passage from Zechariah's prophecy, God declared His jealousy for His people, as well as His intentions to revive them from their season of judgment. "I will save My people from the land of the east and the land of the west. I will bring them back to live in Jerusalem" (Zech. 8:7–8). "As I resolved to treat you badly when your fathers provoked Me to anger, and I did not relent . . . so I have resolved again in these days to do what is good to Jerusalem and to the house of Judah" (vv. 14–15).

And here's how they would know that changes were truly underway. Here are "the things you must do," He said, to begin enjoying all the freedoms of life with Him again: "Speak truth to one another; make true and sound decisions within your gates. Do not plot evil in your hearts against your neighbor, and do not love perjury, for I hate all this" (vv. 16–17).

Something about "truth" lies at the heart of restoration.

"Lord, who can dwell in Your tent," David asked. "Who can live on Your holy mountain?" Answer: "The one who lives honestly, practices righteousness, and acknowledges the truth in His heart—who does not slander with his tongue, who does not harm his friend or discredit his neighbor . . . who keeps his word whatever the cost . . . the one who does these things will never be moved" (Ps. 15:1–5).

Hard question here, coming up—yet also a liberating one. What do you expect would happen, if you *have* been holding something back from confessing or admitting to your spouse—what do you expect would happen if you worked up the spiritual courage to tell them?

Let's answer it this way. With *another* hit of reality. Secrets have a way of coming out. Even if not verbatim, they bubble up in other forms. Just the fact that you're perhaps shielding a side of yourself from your mate—perhaps the full and actual details of a past event—creates an unavoidable wedge of distance between you that cannot, will not, won't ever be knit back together until this blockage is removed. Yes, it might hurt to take it out. Could hurt really bad. For a while. But what God can do amid the healing process can supernaturally forge a stronger bond between the two of you than has ever existed before.

The strain, the break—it won't really go away, not underneath, even if you choose to try keeping it hidden. But the freedom and trust that you and he, or you and she, can finally experience on the other side . . .

Truth is always one of the vital components in making a marriage great. Where has truth been lacking, and how could truth return, so that you can build something even better than you've had?

Day 29

Dare to Not Compare
Being Yourselves

Be satisfied with what you have, for He Himself has said, "I will never leave you or forsake you." (Hebrews 13:5)

I t didn't seem very loving at the time.

Simon Peter and some of the other disciples had been eating breakfast with Jesus—a moment they'd never at all foreseen a month before, when they'd watched in horror as He was hauled away from their presence toward an unjust execution. But amazingly He'd come back to life. And now here He was—like old times.

The bright mood seemed to darken a bit, however, when Jesus began singling out Peter with a pointed, yet confusing series of questions.

"Simon, son of John, do you love Me more than these?" (John 21:15). Three times He asked. And three times Peter answered, "You know that I love You," Lord—the third time with grief in his voice. What did all this mean? Why was Jesus asking him this?

"When you were young," Jesus finally said, "you would tie your belt and walk wherever you wanted. But when you grow old, you will stretch out your hands and someone else will tie you and carry you where you don't want to go" (v. 18). It was an ominous peek into the very real future, when Peter himself would be executed for his loyalty to Christ.

It didn't seem very loving at the time.

Years later, after the Holy Spirit had energized Peter into a solid rock of the early church, he could finally talk about the spiritual connection between "endurance" and "godliness," how it led to a deeper experience of "brotherly affection" and "love"—how "if these qualities are yours and are increasing, they will keep you from being useless or unfruitful in the knowledge of our Lord Jesus Christ" (2 Pet. 1:6–8). He could talk about how "the genuineness of your faith—more valuable than gold, which perishes though refined by fire" can result in a life that gives "praise, glory, and honor" to Christ, how you could experience "inexpressible and glorious joy, because you are receiving the goal of your faith, the salvation of your souls" (1 Pet. 1:7–9).

But at the moment, in the midst of that upsetting conversation, these harrowing words of Jesus mainly struck him with an offended feel of unfairness. *Why me?* At one point, apparently trying to walk off the shock of what he'd heard, Peter looked back and saw his buddy John following a little ways behind. Still processing everything, he swung around to Jesus and said, "Lord—what about him?" (John 21:21). *What's going to happen to him? Are people going to tie him up too? Do terrible things to him too? It's not just me, is it? Why just me?*

Jesus turned to Peter, arresting the full attention of this high-strung follower, and said, "If I want him to remain until I come, what is that to you? As for you, follow Me" (v. 22).

Don't worry about him. Just follow Me.

Looking around today at the situations and circumstances that comprise your life, your marriage, your experience with God—do you ever fail to understand why you've been given some of these things to endure? Why can't you have the much easier, much cushier, much less stressful kind of life that other couples (less deserving couples?) seem to be enjoying?

When God delivered the Ten Commandments to Moses and the people of ancient Israel, He capped off this sacred list with a warning not to "covet your neighbor's house . . . your neighbor's wife" . . . his property, his possessions, "or anything that belongs to your neighbor" (Exod. 20:17). Don't drive by and begrudge them their fancy four-thousand-square-foot house with the three-car garage. Don't huff away in deflated jealousy, after pretending to be excited about your friend's big anniversary trip to New England coming up this summer. Don't lie awake at your husband's snoring tonight and wonder if that cute guy at work, the one who always taps on your desk and says hi when he's walking by, would possibly be capable of making noises like that?

You may really be upset today that your child is needing to go for regular medical therapy after school this afternoon, instead of home to play like other kids are doing. You may be so tired of having to come up with another excuse—again—for why your spouse isn't with you at church this morning, seeing other couples together and happy. You may not be able to believe you'll have to miss going to the game with your buddies on Saturday so you can help your stupid brother-in-law move to his new place, or go to your wife's parents' family reunion at some state park in the country. She promised you'd be there. How many *other* wives would rope their husbands into something like that?

It may not seem loving of God that you're forced to deal with these problems and disappointments—both the major and the minor—while other couples and other families seem so happy and carefree, so settled on a sure path of financial stability and career prominence.

But those who insist on "measuring themselves by themselves and comparing themselves to themselves"—they "lack understanding," Paul said (2 Cor. 10:12). They don't get the message that God has given you *your* life and *your* marriage as your own platform for showing forth His glory. And if you choose to just walk steadily and faithfully through it, not comparing yourself to others, your eyes fixed only on following Him, you will find—as Peter did—that you'll be given "everything required for life and godliness through the knowledge of Him who called us by His own glory and goodness" (2 Pet. 1:3). And your life will be the best life because God has entrusted it to you alone . . . given in love so you can experience Him in your own unique way.

Day 30

I Love You

The Heart of Marriage

These three remain: faith, hope, and love. But the greatest of these is love. (1 Corinthians 13:13)

Sometimes the Bible seems like such an enormous book, the pastor's sermons seem like such impossible challenges, the whole process of growing in Christ and understanding these hard-to-grasp doctrines—it can feel overwhelming, undoable, unknowable. And while the grappling part can actually be a healthy exercise, and while the process of sanctification is sort of intended to make us see our deep dependence on Him, not be impressed by our own spiritual muscle, there are moments when we need to cut through the complexity of it all and simply hear Jesus say . . .

"'Love the Lord your God with all your heart, with all your soul, and with all your mind.' This is the greatest and most important command. The second is like it: 'Love your neighbor as yourself.' All the Law and the Prophets depend on these two commands" (Matt. 22:37–40).

Boil it all down, and that's the Christian life.

Love.

Marriage, too, perhaps once seemed a whole lot simpler. Starting out, everything came so naturally for you. So exciting. New experiences. Embarking on a grand new adventure together. But then it became much more difficult in spots, populated by hurdles and decisions that no one told you about, things you never saw coming. You thought you understood, you thought you'd figured it out, but married life can become surprisingly hard to decode. Being so open, so unguarded, so exposed for the first time . . .

That's why there are moments when the best way to move forward is by sitting back and trying to get the heartbeat of your marriage in view again. Remembering what first drew you together.

Remembering how to love.

When Paul wrote the thirteenth chapter of 1 Corinthians, he probably didn't realize he was writing part of the script for nearly every wedding ceremony that would follow throughout the remainder of history, or was giving copyright-free access to greeting card designers who would transform it into hundreds, thousands, millions of colorful creations. The "love" to which he was speaking is the love that's meant to unify Christian believers with one another, not necessarily just unifying husbands and wives with one another. And yet his poetic portrait of love is certainly descriptive of what can keep our hearts knit together in marriage.

Let's pull it out again. Look at it again.

See what we can learn from it again.

Love is patient. It makes you willing to wait, to dial back your temporary rights and desires, to not put hard dates and times on when something had better happen . . . or else.

Love is kind. It does favors. Picks up after each other. It thinks ahead, seeing something at the store your mate would enjoy and then delighting in being able to bring it home for them.

Love does not envy. It makes you so happy to see your mate succeeding—almost happier than *they* are. You love seeing their dreams come true and seeing other people appreciate them.

Is not boastful. Love doesn't go around comparing your capabilities, demeaning the importance of theirs, thinking how much better you are at doing things . . . the most important things.

Is not conceited. Love won't allow you to be convinced of your own superiority or be dependent on your spouse's praise—being hurt even if they aren't constantly adoring and complimentary.

Does not act improperly. Love minds its manners, is sensitive to the moment, picks up on anything that's causing discomfort or awkwardness, and knows when a joke has gone too far.

Is not selfish. Love helps you patiently learn the value of putting your mate's needs first and helps you recognize the empty result of demanding your own.

Is not provoked. Love doesn't take quick offense, doesn't come in the door ticked off already from something else, but waits to hear the other out, not jumping to conclusions.

Does not keep a record of wrongs. Love forgives. It won't be bringing this instance back up. They won't be hearing about it anymore. You're building a future, not memorializing the past.

Love finds no joy in unrighteousness. Love's desire is to lead each other closer to Christ, more conformed to His character, not stuck in immaturity, conformed to worldly pursuits.

Rejoices in the truth. Love not only tells the truth, but also seeks the truth—the truth of God's Word, the truth of His gospel. It's dead set against being deceived by the lies of the Enemy.

It bears all things. Anything for you, dear. *Believes all things.* Knowing they can do it. *Hopes all things.* Refusing to give up. *Endures all things.* Like a champ.

Love never ends.

This marriage of yours, thirty days older by now, will keep containing some elements that can make it feel hard and complicated sometimes. But here's the simple line you need to be saying and praying as you move on into the next days ahead.

"Love never ends."

Let him know, let her know—somehow, in some way today—that your love will never, ever end.

More from B&H Books

5 Minutes with God in the Car Line
978-1-4336-4570-9
$9.99

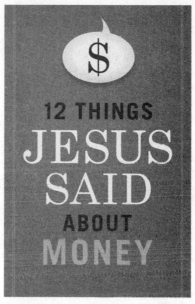

12 Things Jesus Said About Money
978-1-4336-4568-6
$9.99

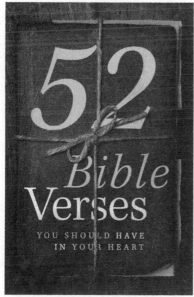

52 Bible Verses You Should
Have in Your Heart
978-1-4336-4569-3
$9.99

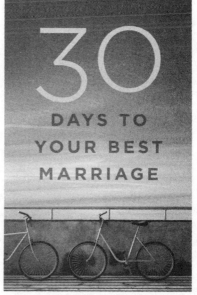

30 Days to Your Best Marriage
978-1-4336-4571-6
$9.99